Writing the Sacred Journey

Writing the Sacred Journey

The Art and Practice of Spiritual Memoir

Elizabeth J. Andrew

SKINNER HOUSE BOOKS
BOSTON

Printed in the United States.

Cover design by Kimberly Glyder.
Author photo by Emily Hughes.
Text design by Suzanne Morgan.

ISBN 1-55896-470-3

Library of Congress Cataloging-in-Publication Data

Andrew, Elizabeth, 1969-
    Writing the sacred journey : the art and practice of spiritual memoir / Elizabeth J. Andrew.
       p. cm.
    Includes bibliographical references.
    ISBN 1-55896-470-3 (alk. paper)
1. Spiritual journals—Authorship. 2. Spiritual biography—Authorship.
3. Autobiography—Authorship. I. Title.

BL628.5.A53 2004
204'.46—dc22

                                                  2004019778

10 9 8 7 6 5 4 3 2 1
06 05 04

We gratefully acknowledge use of the following material:
Excerpt from "East Coker" in *Four Quartets*, copyright 1940 by T. S. Eliot and renewed 1968 by Esme Excerpt Valerie Eliot, reprinted by permission of Harcourt, Inc.
Excerpt from *My Story as Told by Water*, by David James Duncan. Copyright © 2001 by David James Duncan. Reprinted by permission of Sierra Club Books.
Excerpt from *The Confessions of St. Augustine* by John K. Ryan, copyright © 1960 by Doubleday, a division of Random House, Inc. Used by permission of Doubleday, a division of Random House, Inc.
Excerpts from pages 9-12 and 264-65 from *Balancing Heaven and Earth: A Memoir* by Robert A. Johnson and with Jerry M. Ruhl. Reprinted by permission of HarperCollins Publishers Inc.

But whatsoever of the holy kingdom
Was in the power of memory to treasure
Will be my theme until the song is ended.

DANTE, *DIVINE COMEDY*

Contents

Introduction   IX

THE SPIRITUAL MEMOIR

Why We Write   3

The Attributes of Spiritual Memoir   13

Getting Started   24

Inevitable Resistance   27

Developing the Writing Habit   42

The Dilemma of Memory   45

Organizing Your Memories   65

YOUR SPIRITUAL LIFE AS SUBJECT MATTER

Describing the Indescribable   69

The Power of Epiphany   75

Symbols and Metaphors   82

The Vividness of Childhood   88

Being in the Body   100

Honoring Teachers   112

Journeys   123

The Significance of Setting   132

Sharing Suffering   144

The Numinous   155

THE CRAFT OF WRITING

The Power of Showing, The Power of Telling   167

Finding a Structure for Your Story   187

Revision as Seeing Anew   190

Learning to Read as a Writer   218

Putting It Out There   221

Writing Practice, Spiritual Practice   228

For Further Reading   233

Introduction

WHAT, EXACTLY, is spiritual memoir? I was halfway through writing my own before I knew. A mentor began handing me books—wild rides through the Christian faith by Augustine, Teresa of Avila, Margery Kempe, Simone Weil, Thomas Merton, and Henri Nouwen. Later my reading widened to include Sufic, Jewish, Buddhist, Mormon, and New Age memoirs, memoirs by authors of eclectic faiths and authors with no faith tradition at all. I read books by authors who were young, old, famous, unknown, spiritual leaders and ordinary folk, queer and straight, alive and dead. What all these authors had in common was a passionate striving to link their seemingly small lives to some broader truth, some vaster mystery. Although each author's experience of the spiritual was unique, the way each one's experiences emerged in writing was strikingly similar. Familiar themes, structures, and styles appeared across history and culture. Since then, in my work with hundreds of beginning writers, I've come to recognize that the process of writing our sacred stories is filled with common pitfalls and pleasures. Spiritual memoir is a form unto itself.

Philip Zaleski, the editor of Harper SanFrancisco's annual *Best Spiritual Writing* series, defines spiritual writing as "poetry or prose that deals with the bedrock of human existence—why we are here, where we are going, and how we can comport ourselves with dignity along the way." Spiritual memoir, then, is a genre in which one's life is written with particular attention paid to its mysteries. It uses the material of the past and present to ask, What is the source of my existence? What makes me tick? What gives me breath, hope, or inspiration? Invariably spiritual memoir places one's life in relationship to something greater, whether that something be God or oneness or the earth or death. Unlike literary memoir, the purpose of writing spiritual memoir is only secondarily to create a well-crafted work. Spiritual memoirists write because writing brings them nearer to the ineffable essence of life.

This book will teach you how to write memoir with heart and flair; it will help you get started, move through drafts, and gain skills in the craft. That you might learn by others' examples, I've quoted from a variety of memoirists, mostly contemporary, whose stories are accessible and directly helpful to the writing struggle. Underlying all these instructions is an exploration of creative writing as a spiritual practice—a means of opening one's self to transformation and connecting the generative inner sanctum of hope, doubt, and faith to the wider world of community. Language is the bridge. If you write because writing helps you birth yourself, this book is for you.

Throughout the book are writing exercises that are relevant to the accompanying text. However, they needn't be tackled in the order in which they appear. Try both the exercises that inspire you and those that turn you off. A strong emotional reaction (positive or negative) often points toward rich material. Especially do the exercises that seem radically different from your usual approach to writing. You'll find new avenues into the creative process and widen your repertoire. Some of the writing suggestions are brief; others may get you going on an entire book. This diversity is designed to get you started and to teach new techniques, not to overwhelm you with homework. When you find yourself launched on a story, bend the exercise however you wish.

Blessings on you, dear reader, as you travel through this book. May the rigor of learning to write well deepen your insights, widen your relationships, and enlarge the sacred presence you bring into the world.

THE SPIRITUAL MEMOIR

Writing would be merely an act of crazy hubris were
it not a means of discovery, cunning and patient.
—MARY ROSE O'REILLY

Why We Write

WHEN I WAS ATTENDING Sleepy Hollow High School, I'd occasionally forsake the rowdy bus ride home and walk two miles down the steep streets of North Tarrytown, New York, over the infamous bridge where Ichabod Crane is said to have disappeared, and down to the Hudson River. My bookbag weighed against my right shoulder, but my stride was long and increasingly jaunty. By my early teens I'd already been indoctrinated into the relentless race of activities that Americans think compose a well-lived life. My every moment was packed with homework, piano lessons, editing the school literary magazine, volunteering with Girl Scouts, and shelving books at the public library. The rush exhausted me. My walk home became an excuse to disappear from these demands and inhabit the world more freely.

When I came to the river I turned south into our small town park, where the Pocantico River empties into the mighty Hudson and where the little red lighthouse sits proper but dark. There used to be a public beach here, back before lifeguards were required, but the city fenced it off and allowed grapevines and honeysuckle to grow thick between the mowed grass and the sand. Like all the other kids in Tarrytown, I knew that I could still access the beach. I left my books and shoes on the lawn, followed the chain-link fence out along the thin, rocky breakwater; and swung around the end pole, where waves could strike if the river was choppy. The Hudson was steely, lurking between the boulders beneath me. Then it heaved, taking an immense breath. I wrapped my fingers through the chain links to stay balanced.

Once I reached the beach, I jumped down and ran to a log polished silver and reclining on the sand. Here I could have the river to myself—the murky water and the private tuck of shoreline that lay flat like a vast, open palm. In that rare moment of solitude I felt a terrific ache. I wanted to cleave my heart to that dynamic, undulating force that smelled of sea salt and spanned boundless distances. My teenage life was small—fretted with self-consciousness and my peers' misguided expectations. Still, I knew the passion buzzing in my adolescent body was also rolling in that tide. I watched the waves push and pull, and the coarse sand simmer before absorbing the water. I breathed the moist, kelp-scented air. Passion fused me to the river, but there was no release. I was still my lanky, lonely self. I could never dissolve into such magnificence.

What, then, could I do to ease my ache? If I prayed, God's pervasive, dissatisfying silence only intensified my longing. Instead I dug into my jeans' pockets for scrap paper and a ballpoint pen. I did the only thing that transformed my longing into something of substance. I wrote about it.

I no longer have my teenage writing as evidence, but two things remain clear in my memory. One is the inexplicable longing that pushed my pen forward. I remember wanting to burst out of my skin, to become as big on the outside as I felt on the inside. The fact that I was separate from the undulating fabric of the natural world—that I was an independent being—discomfited me. I wanted unity. I wanted to be bound to the tide, to be awash with the created world.

The other thing I remember is that I wrote about what I knew: the river beating against sand, the driftwood hard against my legs, the seagulls holding wind. I wrote my world and, in doing so, felt myself participate fully in its unfolding. I might never accurately describe the salt scent kicked up in the spray, but the attempt changed me; it joined me to the work so evident around me: birthing, changing, destroying, and roiling with beauty.

Today, my drive to write is the same—language, penned to paper, binds the inner world to the outer, satisfying my desire to unite with creation. Why does the effort of translating experience into story satisfy a spiritual need? Over the years I've written three books, countless short memoirs, personal essays, church newsletter columns, poems, and journal entries. I've written myself out of the closet, out of depression, out of regular employment, and into work that fosters a similar passion for writing in others. And still, how writing binds self to creation remains a mystery. I write to find out.

It comforts me that I'm not alone. All sorts of people—elderly church-goers, prisoners, parents, teenage moms, recovering addicts, business executives, homeless people—are eager to put words to their spiritual journeys. Just last week during announcements at a Quaker meeting, a woman in her fifties practically leapt into the air: "I'm finally writing my memoir," she said. "It's amazing! I want to find other people to write with me and talk about it." I recognized in her excitement the impulse that drives us language-lovers to work with our life stories. People seek continuity between the inner world and the outer, between their past selves and who they are now, and especially between what they claim to believe and how they live. Writing helps bring about this continuity. And writing becomes a means to engage that creative force within and beyond us, the sacred presence that lends us life.

The reasons we give for writing spiritual memoirs are often more practical than this abstract, heartfelt longing. We say we want to pass our stories along to our children, or that we need to share our soul's journey with loved ones, or that we want to leave behind more than a financial legacy. Jewish communities in particular are paying increasing attention to the tradition of writing "ethical wills"—documents that place individual lives in a broader context, linking past and future generations by tracing an ethical heritage (see "Writing Resources"). Writing our struggles, our beliefs, and our insights gives us tangible evidence of our internal life to hand to our families.

Another reason people give for writing spiritual memoir is that our experiences have been so transformative, our insights so hard earned, that we feel compelled to share them. One of my students had grown disillusioned with his silk-suit, cell-phone, jet-set lifestyle. After a period of depression, during which he felt his life's efforts had been misdirected and fruitless, he discovered a love of landscaping. If he could write his story, he told me, it might help others transition into lives of greater integrity. Another student saw her mother through hospice care and her final, dying moments. The student's grief was overwhelming, and it seemed the only good she could make of such pain was to write it down in the hope that her story would help others traverse those last days. Wisdom resides inherently within experiences of hardship. Writing is a public manner of claiming this wisdom.

When we write with the professed hope of helping others, I suspect that many of us are really writing for our former selves. The intention to help others is generous; it keeps us motivated and sanctions the huge time investment that writing requires. But what we are writing is the book we wish we had read during our own trying, formative experience. Writing for one's self seems selfish, so we obscure our real motivation with the altruistic desire to help others. In fact, writing for one's self is noble. Each of us is worthy of that generosity. When we return to a difficult period with the care and attention that writing requires, healing happens. Writing connects personal suffering to human suffering, teaching us that we are not alone.

Writing for ourselves, or for our former selves, is more than just a therapeutic exercise. It's essential for writing well. Writing is far too strenuous—too solitary, too sedentary, too emotionally demanding—to sustain if the writer does not somehow benefit from the process. Unfortunately, the benefit rarely comes in the form of money or recognition. We don't live in a culture that values the contemplative remembering or the imaginative labor of making art. And even when our work is publicly received and financially compensated, this recognition rarely satisfies the more profound needs that drive us to write. Love of the grueling work itself, or of the insights that come with it, is necessary to sustain us.

A great many writers are interested in memoir because they understand it to be a spiritual practice. On the surface, writing memoir may seem like a flat transcription of memories, but once you begin writing you discover it is more like call-and-response. You set out to write one funny mishap (say, the time your parents accidentally left you at the gas station during the family vacation) and find yourself reflecting on abandonment. You write your reflections on abandonment, including other memories, and discover a rooted belief that all love entails leaving. When you ask yourself what this might say about the sacred, you feel an onslaught of anger that's been welling since that first mishap. You let your anger rip the page. Upon revision your story grows textured, multilayered.

The balance of expression and receptivity, of solitude and relationship, that emerges from writing provides an opportunity for personal growth. The core reason for writing may not be to generate an end product so much as to engage in the creative process.

THE WRITER'S THREE PRIORITIES

One spring I attended the Festival of Faith and Writing at Calvin College in Grand Rapids, Michigan, and was privileged to hear Jane Yolen speak. Yolen, the author of over a hundred children's books, identified herself as a Jewish Quaker. She spoke on the hazards of addressing spiritual questions in books for children, explaining that children's book buyers are primarily public schools and libraries, which tend to shy away from spiritually inclined literature. Nonreligious publishers are often unwilling to take on material that might prove controversial. Yet as Yolen pointed out, children ask spiritual questions: Where did Rover go when he died? Why do some people attend church and not others? Who is God? Yolen argued that we do wrong by our children when we censor stories that might aid them in their seeking.

After Yolen's lecture a member of the audience asked, "To whom do you think children's authors should be accountable for the moral quality of their books?" The questioner was concerned that indoctrinating content might wind up in her children's hands. Yolen responded fiercely, "Every writer has three responsibilities: first to the story, second to yourself, and finally to your audience."

I often think about Yolen's three commandments. Although they apply to all creative writing, they hold particularly true for spiritual memoir. Thinking first about the audience rather than about the story or about yourself is a frequent but misguided habit among beginning writers. At some point (about draft three or four), it's important to be accountable to your audience. You want your story to be welcoming, accessible, gripping, and transformative. Considering your reader's response helps you construct a story that accomplishes these things.

But through the early stages of writing, your primary audience is yourself. Write to satisfy you. If you think first about your readers (about what you have to teach them, whether or not they'll buy the book, or if they will like or condemn your message), you begin to mold your writing to your expectation of readers' reactions. You do a disservice to yourself when you avoid risky topics or skirt deep levels of honesty.

What intrigues me about Jane Yolen's priorities—and why I believe them to be particularly relevant to spiritual memoir—is her placement of the story first. What does it mean to be responsible to the story? For writers of spiritual memoir, story is not something born of the imagination or of history; it is the very stuff of our lives. It is the aching and questing of our souls. Although seemingly mundane, ordinary experiences contain within them a vivacity, a sense of wholeness, and a will beyond our own. In other words, our spiritual stories bare the world's holiness. This ought to be obvious, but religious traditions of all persuasions have a tendency to canonize certain stories and certain people's lives. In the process of honoring these stories, we forget to honor the revelatory qualities of our own stories. When memoir writers are responsible to the story, they honor that which is vital and true—the spirit—within their experience.

When you are chatting idly with the neighbor and she asks you whom you're writing for, it's easier to say "readers who are struggling with grief" than it is to say "me!" But there is a third, more subtle answer—one that is at the source of your drive and conviction: "I write for the story itself." Of course, you don't say this to the neighbor because she would think you're crazy. Writers rarely even acknowledge it to themselves. But the answer is there nonetheless, prodding writers along. How many hundreds of times have writers declared, "My story needs to be told"? And it does—for its own bare sake. We are compelled by our encounters with pain, doubt, rebellion, and revelation to dialogue with these memories and release them from the bonds of our bodies onto the page. Even an unpublished, unread memoir exerts influence on the world. Stories, in and of themselves, *matter*.

> ∾ *In* The Names, *N. Scott Momaday writes about one of his characters, "He thought of it as the one time in his life to which we would willingly return from any and all other times; it was simply the best of his memories." Write down your best memory for the simple sake of treasuring it.*

You can only discover why a story matters by telling or writing it. Even then the story's reason for emerging remains a mystery. Perhaps you have seen evidence that a story can have a will of its own. You begin with the intention of writing about your meditation teacher's soothing voice and end up describing your grandmother's bedtime songs and what a terrible loss you felt when your family moved far away from her. Your job as memoirist is to listen to what your stories tell you. It's only through revision and contemplation that you learn that your grandmother is at the center of the story, and that she taught you to trust the quiet moment before sleep. We think we know our stories, but in fact they have a tremendous capacity to surprise and teach us. Work long enough with a memory and it will exert its silent, irascible will.

A story's will can be especially strong when others (individuals or society) have denied its existence, covered over the truth with other stories, or forbidden the story to be told. When working with writers of color, queer writers, or women writers raised in patriarchal faiths who are finding their voices for the first time, I am struck by how forcefully their stories drive them to write. Writing becomes necessary, not just for the individual but for the culture as a whole.

I work with a woman writer who has a beard. Daily she is harassed and abused by strangers who are unsettled by her body's lack of conformity. She has written her way through a locked psychiatric ward and subsequent years of depression and is now asserting her natural self's place in the world by writing her story. The glossy advertising billboards and harassers will not have the final say. Her story needs to be told.

When I consider the value that Western culture places on material things; when I encounter advertising's perpetual message that we need to change ourselves to be acceptable, happy, or loved; and when I notice how difficult it is to squeeze a walk into my day or to quiet my mind's perpetual chatter, I see that the spiritual life itself has become marginalized, even oppressed. So many demands run roughshod over the soul's needs that we often forget those needs exist. The activities that most nourish the spirit (play, affection, generosity, contemplation, quiet, beauty, creativity, truth-telling, time in nature) are least valued in a consumer society. Spending a morning with a pen and notepad, traversing the landscape of memory and searching for the sacred, is a profoundly countercultural activity. No wonder the impulse to probe the spiritual life with language presses against so many people's hearts. That neglected dimension of self is rebelling—insisting that its story come into the light.

Writing, then, becomes a way of attending to life's submerged currents. Anne Frank expresses this in her diary when she says, "I want to write, but more than that I want to bring out all kinds of things that lie buried in my heart." Frank had an inherent love of language and followed that affection in the locked pages of her diary. She understood that writing was a bridge between the secret, wealthy realm of her being and the external world. Albert Einstein puts it another way: "The greatness of an artist lies in the building of an inner world, and in the ability to reconcile this inner world with the outer." Language accesses and translates that which pulses, inexplicably, through our bloodstreams. It is simultaneously a way in and a way out.

When we write down a spiritual journey for its own sake, we become responsible to the story itself—to the sacred story. The longing I felt as a teenager sitting beside the Hudson River; indeed, the longing I feel today, poised at the keyboard, is the press of the Sacred yearning to emerge. When we write, we help bring holiness to birth. Writing is a way to participate in the world and in its continued creation.

The Attributes of Spiritual Memoir

THREE QUALITIES MAKE the genre of spiritual memoir unique: The spir- *k*
itual writer uncovers, probes, and honors what is sacred in his or her life
story; the writing process itself is a means to spiritual growth; and the
end product makes the experience of the sacred available to the reader.

The heart of spiritual memoir is intensely private. It is an intimate *k*
conversation between the writer and a great mystery. In traditional
spiritual memoir, authors even veer from the story to praise or address
the sacred in prayer. "How hidden you are," Augustine wails in his
Confessions, "you who dwell on high in silence, you the sole great
God!" Teresa of Avila felt God waiting for her story, addressing God
from the outset in her *Life of Saint Teresa*: "I pray Him with all my
heart for the grace to write this account . . . The Lord, too, I know, has
long desired that it should be written, but I have never been bold
enough to begin. May it be to His glory and praise."

We see a similar impulse in contemporary memoir, when authors
raise ruthless questions, grapple with awe and suffering, and persis-
tently attempt to describe the indescribable. The following passage
from Peter Matthiessen's *The Snow Leopard*, which tells of his journey
with field biologist George Schaller to the Himalayas, illustrates this

struggle to put mystery into words. A Nepalese scientist confronts Matthiessen:

> He could understand why GS, as a biologist, would walk hundreds of miles over high mountains to collect wildlife data on the Tibetan Plateau. But why was I going? What did I hope to find?
>
> I shrugged, uncomfortable. To say I was interested in blue sheep or snow leopards, or even in remote lamaseries, was no answer to his question, though all of that was true; to say I was making a pilgrimage seemed fatuous and vague, though in some sense that was true as well. And so I admitted that I did not know. How could I say that I wished to penetrate the secrets of the mountains in search of something still unknown that, like the yeti, might well be missed for the very fact of searching?

However it manifests itself, in spiritual memoir the author's engagement with mystery is always at the fore.

> ☙ *Describe a small, ordinary activity that you've already done today (brushing your teeth, buckling your seatbelt, etc.). Imagine that this event appears in your spiritual memoir. Reflect: What does this activity reveal about you? What mystery does it contain? No subject lacks the potential to reveal the spiritual.*

Every spiritual memoir reaches into mystery, attempting to place human life in a broad sacred context. Your task as a writer is not to shy from the unknown but to interact with it, to stretch your hand forward into the abyss. This is the second distinguishing attribute of spiritual memoir: The writing itself becomes a means for spiritual growth. Often the writer stumbles on this strange occurrence middraft, discovering that the writing itself is an avenue for prayer, a means of wrestling with angels, or a form of contemplation.

Once you experience writing as an agent of spiritual growth, it's possible—indeed, fruitful—to invite growth every time you sit down to write. Take, for instance, the following introduction to Nancy Mairs' memoir, *Ordinary Time*:

> I have spent the whole of my conscious life—against all principles of reason—in an uneasy and unrelenting state of religious faith, and as I hurtle toward the half-century mark, I find myself wanting with increasing urgency to know why and how I've done such a thing and what the consequences have been. The only way I can find out is through language, learning line by line as the words compose me. Other people may have developed different and more efficient strategies, but in order to know anything at all, I have to write a book.

Or consider May Sarton's speculation in *Journal of Solitude*: "Perhaps we write towards what we will become from where we are." Many writers say they write to discover what they think. For some of us, the wiring of our brains is such that only the written word can bring clarity. Those who write spiritual memoir write to find out what we believe or, more fundamentally, what we know to be sacred and true. The rough draft of your spiritual story lays experience out in a manageable fashion. In subsequent drafts, as you hone details, smooth transitions, and work to create an artistic whole out of your stories, the experiences become unified and tangible. Writing, especially revision, enables you to delve into layers of symbolism, dissonance, and purpose. By writing down your sacred story, you may glimpse its entirety. Awareness that the soul's journey is bound to the writing journey shines clearly through all compelling spiritual memoir.

When writers are open to learning and growing through the writing process, a sense of discovery infuses our words. Personal growth isn't a selfish reason for writing; it's an essential ingredient in effective stories. As Robert Frost puts it, "No surprise for the writer, no surprise for the reader." The reader latches on to our experience of vulnerability and risk, following our growth like a lead-rope.

Teachers often admonish beginning writers, "Write what you know!" It's good advice. The wisdom we know deep inside ourselves is infinitely richer than anything we can be taught. In memoir, you blatantly write what you know. Your memories are your subject; the story already exists, and you are simply transcribing it onto the page. At least that's the way it seems before you start writing. But not that far into your draft you discover that you know much less than you thought. What really happened? What do these memories reveal about you or about the sacred? Why, after all, are you writing?

When I lived at a retreat center secluded in the woods, the guests who came from the cities would occasionally take walks at night. They would shut the front door, walk the length of the well-lit porch, and face the unfamiliar, looming darkness of Norwegian pines, ironwood, and oak. Many later reported that they could not go further: They couldn't see well enough or felt afraid of what lurked in the woods. Some, however, took a few bold steps down to the driveway. Just before the darkness swallowed them, a shock of light flooded the drive, set off by a motion detector. The adventurers could safely proceed another forty feet before darkness again conquered their vision. Then another light flashed on. Three times between the house and the road, lights sensed their movement and steered them forward. Once they were on the road, even a cloudy sky provided enough light to proceed.

Over breakfast the next morning, these guests shared their surprise. "You have to take a few steps into the dark, just trusting," one said, "before another light shows the way."

The Quakers call this "proceeding as the way opens," and it's good counsel for writers as well as spiritual seekers. Often the way is draped in shadow and we must proceed anyhow. It is common for the beginning of a writing project to be paved and well lit. A topic propels you out of the house; you're determined, curious, or on a mission. But it's not long before the porch light recedes. Our writing peters out; our energy fades, and the direction we were so sure about suddenly seems ill-advised. The trouble with writing about what we know is that our story is constrained by the limits of our knowledge—we can only go as far as the pool of porch light. How can we take those few tentative steps beyond the first rim of light into the wooded darkness?

Spiritual memoir entails moving forward by writing what we *don't* know—writing our way into the mystery. "I haven't a clue as to how my story will end," Nancy Willard writes. "But that's all right. When you set out on a journey and night covers the road, you don't conclude that the road has vanished. And how else could we discover the stars?"

    ⁊ *Consider a simple memory that haunts you. Make two lists: what you know and what you don't know about the memory. What items from each list interest you most? Write a short paragraph reflecting on the two items.*

While arriving at the edge of what's obvious can be terrifying (often we're overly eager to label it "writer's block"), it is in fact a rich opportunity. If we can muster our strength and take the first few stumbling steps forward, our writing often gains an unexpected dimension. The brain is forced to step down as the primary tour guide, and the gut takes a far more unprofessional lead. Of course, this makes us uncomfortable. The gut is apt to digress wildly into subjects we're not prepared to tackle. The gut is obsessed with secrets, unresolved emotions, and darkness. But it's terribly important to trust the gut and follow its meanderings. Some may prove to be red herrings, but others steer us deeper into the heart of the matter—a heart we didn't know was there.

୧ *Write down a question that you wish you knew the answer to. Then write a memory that helps explain the origin of the question. What happened that made this question important? As you write, pay attention to how the story illuminates the question.*

It's one thing to give voice to a story and quite another to address an audience so others can receive the story's gifts, which brings me to the third defining characteristic of spiritual memoir: The writer works to tell his or her story in such a way that the experience of the sacred is made available to the reader. When you take time to craft your work—revising it, finding thematic threads, developing scenes, smoothing over transitions, and uncovering the story's inherent unity—you invite readers into your world. You help them experience what you've experienced. A well-crafted work welcomes readers, takes their hats and coats, and gives them a thorough tour of the house. The readers then feel at ease enough to dwell in the story for awhile and perhaps be changed by it.

Most people setting out to write memoir don't have literary aspirations. Yet learning the craft of writing brings rich insight about the past and about one's relationship with mystery. The process of shaping and deepening a draft helps satisfy the fundamental longing for connection. The rigor of learning to write well—not just getting the story down but giving it a pleasing form—extends our insights, enlarges our thinking, and widens the scope of our world. When we craft stories for an audience, whether or not an audience will ever read them, we discover the many gifts of revision. We discover how the self is revised along with our writing.

"Most good stories are mysteries," Bliss Broyard writes. "The author is like a detective trying to get to the bottom of some truth." As odd as it may seem, moving away from the assumption that you know your material can make the sacred part of it more accessible to your readers. Think of memoir writing as mystery writing. Your first draft is a write-up of the crime scene, suspects, and clues. You are a detective chasing your subject. What unknown entity lurks at the center of your story? Why is this quest important to you? Why might it be important to others?

The centerpiece of your story may not be a murder, but it is certainly something essential and human. What pieces of evidence are conspicuously missing? Perhaps the protagonist (you) didn't want to disclose them in the first draft. Now you must drag out those memories, look up those witnesses, and bring to light what's been in shadows in order to make sense of the story. What is the telling evidence that points to your story's heart? Take those scenes and expand them, noting every detail, as a way of listening to their clues. Your job is to uncover the central act of passion that brought together these people, objects, and emotions in a single place.

Whether or not the solution to the mystery becomes clear at the end is irrelevant; what makes a good memoir is the search, not the resolution. In *Letters to a Young Poet*, Rainer Maria Rilke gives similar advice to a young poet who feels himself to be erring with "words when they are meant to mean most delicate and almost inexpressible things":

> Be patient toward all that is unsolved in your heart and try to love the *questions themselves* like locked rooms and like books that are written in a very foreign tongue. Do not now seek the answers, which cannot be given you because you would not be able to live them. And the point is, to live everything. *Live* the questions now. Perhaps you will then gradually, without noticing it, live along some distant day into the answer.

If you are able to reside within your questions, if you allow memories to speak their mysteries, then the Great Mystery breathes life into your story. Only then will it touch your reader.

> ❧ *Make a list of all the grand questions of your life. (What happens when we die? Why did your mother abandon you? What exactly does it mean to forgive?) Add to this list questions about the minute mysteries in life (Why do people hiccup? How will I get the phone bill paid?). Reflect on what it means to love these questions.*

In a way, the three attributes of spiritual memoir are Jane Yolen's three priorities within a sacred context. Those who write spiritual memoir pursue mystery—inside the story, within themselves, and for their readers.

Memoir's Small Frame

Memoir revolves in an orbit of its own choosing, and therefore its pieces are often unified by a theme or period of time. The material is always the author's life, and the narrator, (the speaker, or "I" voice), is always the author. Unlike autobiography, which attempts as complete an account of one's life as possible, starting from the beginning, memoir begins where it wishes and concludes when its story is told. Memoir is more elastic, unpredictable, and crafted than autobiography. Because memoir does not strive for a complete accounting of one's life, it depends on other elements, typically themes, to give it form.

> *What are some of the grand themes of your life (abandonment, coming out, fear, courage, letting go)? What are the questions that you ponder when you wake up at night (or that recur in your journal) that you wish you could ask others about at potlucks or over tea? Make a list. The grand themes of your life become the grand themes of your memoir.*

Because memoir, by its very nature, is only a small window into the author's life, one of the delights of writing memoir is discovering the best frame for that window. I remember an afterschool art class in which we were given a view finder (a black cardboard mat of about six square inches with a one-inch square hole cut in the center). We walked into the woods holding our view finders in front of our faces, looking for a view. Eventually I found a mossy root that entered and exited that small window in a way that intrigued me, and I sat down with a sketchbook to draw it. Memoir is similar. A small scope is all that's necessary. Some memoirists choose to write only about their depression, or their travels, or their cultural identity. Spiritual memoirists choose their sacred journeys. You can select a significant portion of your life, or a few years, or a single day. Regardless of the frame, some material comes into focus and other material—the majority of the woods, in fact—is left out of the picture. And that's okay. Despite my drawing's small scope, it conveyed the lush and creeping wooded environment. Whatever cross-section of life you choose to portray reveals the essence of the whole.

The peculiar and thrilling thing about framing is how much control it gives you, and also how little. As an author you decide what appears inside the frame and what does not. If you're most interested in exploring how your family's religious traditions affected your childhood spirit, you don't have to disclose your recent divorce or ninth-grade sports injury. Scott Russell Sanders' short memoir "Amos and James" explores his childhood obsession with the Bible, which was fed by a difficult family life. Sanders wants the reader to know why he read so voraciously without having to explain the family's problems. And so he draws a line:

> Reading Amos was like listening through the closed door of my bedroom to my parents quarreling. The words were muffled, but the fierce feelings came through.
>
> Why my parents fought is another story, and a long one, featuring too much booze and too little money. For this story, I can only say that their shouts and weeping drove me to scour the Bible at age twelve in search of healing secrets.

Indeed, Sanders has written elsewhere about his father's alcoholism. Here he exposes the edges of his frame, what he is and isn't allowing the reader to see. Sanders lets us know only as much as is necessary to understand his relationship with the Bible, the subject at hand.

Although you control what is visible in your memoir and what remains hidden, ultimately the content is *not* your decision. The story itself has the final say and often dictates directions you would rather not go. You may want to write about your relief at finding a church home, but in order for that story to make sense you must include the decade of disconnection and searching that preceded it. Or you may want to honor your grandmother by describing how she knit mittens for all the kids at the neighborhood center, but you are reminded of finding mittens with horrible, misshapen thumbs in her basket after she died. You may find that your real story isn't simple or happy. Although memoir allows many creative choices regarding what you write and how you write it, the story always holds you accountable.

Spiritual memoir demands the truth. The story of a spiritual life has a will of its own, and you write in its service.

Getting Started

WRITE A LITTLE EVERY DAY. Often the biggest hurdle for beginning writers is getting the butt in the chair. That sounds callous, but it's true—discipline is terrifically hard. And yet new writers make it harder than necessary. You needn't produce a treatise with every sitting. In fact, it's better to start small—ten minutes a day—and build from there once you desire more. Over time it's astonishing how much writing you can produce in short bursts. Set a timer and stop when the timer goes off. A clear time frame can make the task of writing less daunting and allow for some wonderful work.

Create writing rituals. Find a favorite pen, notebook, and chair. Light a candle. Go to that same corner café. Ritual is an invitation, a way of saying to the world, "I'm here! I'm paying attention!" If you show up, the muse will meet you. For some people, an important part of the ritual is writing at the same time every day. Writing is as much a part of my morning as brushing my teeth and drinking tea. This way, writing is assumed—of course I write! I wouldn't skip my toothbrush or tea, and so I never skip writing, either.

Be messy. Your first order of business is to generate material. Get those memories and reflections out of your head. Don't censor. Write whatever comes to you, even if it's not what you originally set out to write about. "Judgment," poet Richard Broderick writes, "is the death of the imagination." Be gentle with yourself. There is always time later to focus and clean up your writing. What emerges on the page is a first draft; it will evolve a lot before it is final. In the meanwhile, take advantage of the terrific freedom to make mistakes with content and mechanics (spelling, grammar, etc.). Be wild and fearless. A careful first draft hinders spontaneity. A genuinely rough draft opens possibilities.

Be on the lookout for ideas. When a memory flashes through your body, take note. It's a gift. Write it down! You are not just a writer when you're sitting at the computer. You are a writer every moment of the day inasmuch as you look out for inspiring ideas, memories, and reflections. Keep pen and paper with you at all times. Ideas are temperamental; they betray you if you're not paying attention.

Keep a writer's journal. Either on the computer or in a notebook, keep an ongoing journal of ideas, quotations, ponderings, anecdotes, memories, and other miscellany that comes your way. This journal can serve as a dumping ground for false starts that might otherwise go into the trash or as a place for thrashing through writer's block, asking, Why am I stumped? What might I be afraid of? What do I really want to write? No one but you will ever see your journal. You can be fearlessly messy, explore risky questions, and experiment with your prose without endangering the actual manuscript of your memoir. The journal serves as a catch-all for the language crumbs of your project.

Be on the lookout for the edge. Sometimes a good idea isn't enough to get you going. You need to discover the edge—what nags you, what you really want to ask strangers at the bus stop, what you ponder when you can't sleep at night. The edge is the theme that recurs in your journal. The edge is your most secret doubt. Often you can find the edge by asking, What am I not writing about? The subjects you avoid have spunk; avoidance is evidence of their power. If you are afraid to write about sex or money or relationships, chances are good those subjects have an energy that will serve you well. If this edge seems unrelated to your memoir, remember that the questions that haunt you invariably haunt your writing. The edge is the heart question that drives you to put pen to paper in the first place.

Don't fret about organization. Start with whatever memory moves you and follow your interest. If it's helpful to write your story in chronological order, go for it. If it helps to collect anecdotes around a common subject, such as influential people in your life or all the places of worship you've visited, do that. Your first job is to amass material. By virtue of being human, certain themes and questions run like veins of gold through the rock of your being. First drafts are just the beginning stages of mining. As you start digging, trust that your memoir's organization will emerge organically from within your accumulated writing.

Find a writing community. Writing doesn't have to be a lonely business. A writing group or writing partner can help you stay motivated, provide you with deadlines, and support you through the more grueling stages. Surrounding yourself with creative people on journeys similar to your own reminds you of how worthy the work is. A safe, supportive community can be a huge inspiration during a difficult process.

Inevitable Resistance

THE HARDEST PART about writing memoir is maintaining a daily discipline. Even if the ideas are flying a mile a minute, even if you can think of nothing else you'd rather do with your life, even if you love language spilling from your pen, it's still a challenge to sit down and work. Resistance springs up like weeds—naturally and in abundance. You can let resistance win and give up writing altogether or you can learn to mulch, spend hours on your knees, and tolerate a few dandelions between tomato plants.

Who has the time to write? From my writing chair I can easily see a dozen household projects—the porch needs sweeping, the bird feeders ought to be filled, papers litter the floor of my office. And then there are the lesson plans I haven't written, the e-mail that is only a click away, and other more lucrative responsibilities. I am an outrageously slow writer. The average time it takes me to produce a book of creative prose is six years. The trouble with writing is that most of us have to earn an income alongside this crazy compulsion, or raise a family, or care for elderly parents. We need to carry on with *living*. In comparison, writing about living seems somehow wasteful.

If time is not the problem, there's bound to be another reason not to write. No ideas? No audience? No clear direction? Maybe you space out in front of the computer screen, your mind a temporary, blissful blank. Or you find your own words repugnant. Or what emerges is a pale shadow of your brilliant idea, and the disappointment is unbearable. Who, after all, cares?

There are a thousand reasons not to begin or to suddenly abort the writing process. Not having enough time is by far the most ubiquitous. As real as these reasons may be, when push comes to shove, they are just excuses. If you really want to write, you can make the time, you can bear the ugliness of your words, you can write through your own dissatisfaction. Toni Morrison wrote her first novels while she was a single mother and working full time as an editor. Christopher Paul Curtis wrote the Newbery Award-winning novel *Bud, Not Buddy* while working the factory line. David Bayles and Ted Orland, authors of *Art and Fear*, warn that "Uncertainty is the essential, inevitable and all-pervasive companion to your desire to make art. And tolerance for uncertainty is the prerequisite to succeeding." Novelist Michael Cunningham puts it even more directly: "A certain fearlessness in the face of your own ineptitude is a useful tool." One page each weekday makes the draft of a short book in a year. As rotten as that draft may be, another year of revision makes it palatable, and a third year makes it positively desirable. If you have the urge to write and it continues to nag at you, regardless of your excuses, any long-term reason for not writing is bunk. It's not a reason. It's a form of resistance.

Resistance, unfortunately, is inevitable. For one thing, we live in a culture that balks at the seeming idleness of creativity. Most of us have swallowed this value without serious critical thought. We adore final products and lift best-selling authors onto pedestals while dismissing no-names who are knee-deep in their writing (ourselves included). The pages that wind up between two covers are the same manuscript pages that have been labored over in privacy and agony; they are worthy of reverence long before a publisher notices them. We resist the process because we're too eager for the product and cannot see that a mere fifteen minutes a day makes headway in reaching that goal. It does. It makes the difference between writing and not writing. We resist the process because it is hard work. Moments of muse-induced, free flow are few. Most days writing is grueling, and it's a rare soul who wouldn't avoid such a gut-wrenching chore.

Underlying every measly excuse for not writing is unremitting resistance to growth. Writing makes terrifying demands. You must remember, vividly, moments that hold sway over you and that, for this very reason, you would prefer to keep buried. You're forced to consider the possibility—indeed, the likelihood—that what you have set out to write is merely an illusion and that some unknown, more potent purpose lurks two pages ahead. Writing makes you vulnerable. It exposes weaknesses; it reopens wounds. It lays imperfections bare. We all fear being exposed, but the truer fear is the fear of the transformation inherent in writing: We fear our creative power. We shudder at the potential influence of our own voices. And when the subject matter is the very ground of our being, it is likely that writing will affect that ground, turn its soil, and plant its outrageous seeds.

Early in my writing career, I attended a women's writing retreat on the north shore of Lake Superior. Each writer stayed in a writing shack in the woods. I swung open the squeaky door to mine to find an ideal writing space: a large window overlooking the lake; a wide, empty desk; a rocker and reading lamp; an extravagant dictionary; and a monster box of tissues. I remember the tissues because I used reams during the following seven days and felt grateful to the hospitality angel who had foreseen my need.

In hindsight I see that this writing shack, even though I only wrote there for a week, did me unlimited long-term good. It taught me that hundreds of writers before and after me needed those tissues to do their best writing. The size of that tissue box was a testimony to the emotional work writing requires. It reminded me of how Sherry Ruth Anderson and Patricia Hopkins, the authors of *The Feminist Face of God*, describe resistance to the spiritual journey:

> When we are on the verge of making a deep promise, it is not uncommon for great resistances and fears to arise. Whatever threatens our reality or present way of life, whatever we know will profoundly change us, often seems more terrifying than inviting. But if we are able to make the commitment, we sometimes experience an unexpected joy.

My wastebasket was full of wadded tissues. I had found a joyful place in a lineage of writers.

Resisting writing, then, is not unlike resisting other spiritual practices. Certainly there are good reasons for not practicing—we don't have time, the posture is hard on the body, it doesn't make a measurable difference—and every reason is a mechanism for dodging inner change. Isak Dinesen gives this advice: "Write a little every day, without hope and without despair." Her words remind me of T. S. Eliot's passage from *The Four Quartets*:

✦ I said to my soul, be still, and wait without hope

For hope would be hope for the wrong thing; wait without
    love
For love would be love of the wrong thing; there is yet faith
But the faith and the love and the hope are all in the waiting.

Writing without hope or despair is a manner of waiting in what Eliot calls "the still point of the turning world." It's a way of inhabiting the heart of creation, the very nexus of being. Hope—for publication, for making high art, for writing something wise—is hope for the wrong thing, and it gets in the way. Despair—over your inadequacies or lack of readership or ordinary life—is also a needless hindrance. Wait. And write. Faith, love, and hope reside in the process.

There is no cure for resistance except to write. Write about your resistance; enter into conversation with it, ask it what it wants to say, find out its origin and history. If you get on speaking terms with your resistance, it can teach you important things. Certainly you have wisdom to teach it.

    In the center of a piece of paper, sketch an image or write the name of your inner critic. Radiating outward, write the many messages that critic gives you while you're writing. Be sure to include the good messages that are really wolves in sheep's clothing ("Your mother will be so proud!") along with the obviously harmful messages ("What are you thinking?" or "Who do you think you are, anyway?"). Once you've exhausted your critic's repertoire, sort through them. Identify which messages are helpful but untimely ("You can't spell!" or "Your words are so bland!") and tell the critic that you'll attend to these concerns later, when it's time to revise. Then identify the messages that are downright destructive. Dialogue with these messages. Ask where they come from and why they persist. Write in your journal about their origins. The point is to not fight your inner critic as you are writing, wasting precious time and energy. If you allow the critic to speak fully, you can thank it for its input and move on.

Eventually, by writing through your resistance, you can train it to behave. When you are doing the dishes or commuting to work, your resistance to writing can romp freely. But when you're at the writing desk, resistance needs to heel and roll over. It's not worth the effort to try to banish resistance; for most people this is impossible and perhaps even undesirable. When resistance nudges you, usually it's a sign that you're on to something good. The stronger your resistance, the greater potential there is for discovery.

   🙰 *Consider a subject that makes you feel a great deal of resistance (perhaps anxiety about your relationship with a member of your family or about a moment of physical vulnerability). Begin writing with the sentence, "I don't want to write about . . . because. . . ." Go into as much detail as you can.*

Kathleen Norris writes in *Dakota*, "Fear is not a bad place to start a spiritual journey. If you know what makes you afraid, you can see more clearly that the way out is through the fear." Likewise with resistance: If you thwart its siren call of distraction and instead move into and through your internal rebellion, resistance becomes an invaluable guide.

Who Cares? Audience and Ego

"She didn't read books," Zora Neale Hurston writes about her character, Janie, in Their Eyes Were Watching God, "so she didn't know that she was the world and the heavens boiled down to a drop."

Poor Janie! Uneducated, deprived of literature, she thought she was just a woman walking around her Florida town. But Zora Neale Hurston knew otherwise. Each of us is a concentrated universe; each of us mirrors eternity. Books and stories demonstrate this amazing phenomenon.

When you find yourself asking, Who am I to write this story? Why would anyone care? remember Janie, and know that you, too, are "the world and the heavens boiled down to a drop." Then consider why you read memoir, especially ordinary people's memoirs. Often the answers are variations on a theme: You like experiencing others' lives vicariously; you learn how others deal with problems similar to your own; you sense a truth in others' stories and so can recognize the truth within your own.

Why then should these not be the answers for your story as well? The universe is packed into your very cells; the molecules of your body are made of stardust flung from the Big Bang. Think of yourself as holographic, every fragment of your being containing the whole universe. Your pain taps into the world's suffering, your laughter at a bad joke is a human release, and your bout of loneliness reveals creation's drive for connection. You may not have climbed Mount Everest or served as President of the United States; you may not have suffered severe sexual abuse or been tortured by an oppressive government; you may not have taken religious vows or achieved enlightenment; you may be twenty-four years old, or forty-six, or ninety-two; indeed, the scope of your life and insights may seem exceptionally narrow. And still your story has inherent worth. The challenge is to uncover value where you presume none.

There's a simple writing exercise I love to do with my classes. I ask everyone to write his or her story of taking out the garbage. Can you find a more mundane topic? For ten minutes we scribble away, describing what seems to have no merit whatsoever. Even after we're done, the writers feel their work is pedantic. Then we go around the circle and read aloud what we've written. One woman has a shiny lid on her kitchen can, on top of which she places a paper bag because it's too much work to open the lid every time she tosses a banana peel. One man discusses how his trash has been reduced since he started composting; now he hauls buckets to the backyard. A young woman writes that, living with her parents, she has never taken out the trash; even in her car, she tosses all the gum wrappers and soda cans into the back seat. Still another student tells how he races outside at six in the morning in his bathrobe and slippers when he hears the truck rumbling down the alley. From the diversity of stories, it becomes clear that no two of us have the same attitude toward our garbage. Our little anecdotes reveal the most unlikely personality traits. They confirm Lynne Sharon Schwartz's bit of wisdom: "There's nothing new under the sun except the sound of another voice."

Then I push the exercise further. I ask everyone to consider the story's driving question, image, or issue. Sure it's about garbage, but what else is it about? Procrastination? The abundance of waste? Fear of letting go? Write this theme at the top of the page, and then rewrite your garbage piece with this in mind. No matter how dull it appears, anything at all—even garbage—can be an avenue into heart and meaning.

❧ Choose a task from your to-do list (mowing the lawn, shopping for groceries, mopping the kitchen). Describe what it will be like to perform the chore. How will it feel to do the job? Why does it matter? What is your history with this chore? What does it reveal about your values and beliefs?

Without a doubt the universal is contained in the particular. Every story has inherent worth. Even knowing this, too many writers are haunted by the question, Who cares? Some never begin writing because this question, unanswered, stops them cold. Too many of us have given our validation rights over to others. Someone else (the market economy, the publisher, the grant review board, the neighbors, readers, a parent) has been given the authority to determine your worth—through how much he or she pays you or publicizes you or affirms you with kisses.

The inability to trust our own intrinsic worth is rampant. Perhaps it's because Americans are plagued hourly with advertising that tells us that we would be worthy if only we had a red sports utility vehicle with a sun roof and heated seats and a garage to park it in and. . . . Perhaps we are unable to tap internal wealth because it is countercultural. No one will pay you to pray. An hour spent dreaming in the woods with a pen and pad doesn't count as productive use of time. We are constantly steered away from our own wisdom and stories toward something elusive we must hurry to find elsewhere.

The "Who cares?" question assumes writing to be a product, valuable inasmuch as others are willing to consume it. But writing is a product only at the tail end of a long and arduous process. The writing process, like any spiritual journey, is worthwhile for its own sake. The only answer to the "Who cares?" question that really matters is whether or not you care. Do you care enough to believe in your story, to invest time in your memories, to work hard, to continue to learn? Do you care whether your story has a life outside of your head? Creative writing of any sort requires care, but spiritual memoir requires it of our very souls. Do you care enough to seek out the sacred in your story?

There's another subtle assumption behind the "Who cares?" question that wields great power. We ask, Who cares? because we assume that memoir shines the spotlight on *self*. On the surface, self does appear to be memoir's subject. But the real subject of autobiographical writing is not self so much as human consciousness. Self is simply a tool to access broader questions and themes. In other words, I offer up the character that is me, as real and accurate as I can make it, in the service of whatever gives me life and breath. Self is a means to an end. As George Bernard Shaw puts it, "The man who writes about himself and his own time is the only man who writes about all people and about all time." When you write spiritual memoir, the spotlight shines through the self to the mystery behind it, to questions about the meaning of suffering, to the puzzle of embodiment or the search for forgiveness. Memoir is not about the author after all.

I'd like to pose an alternative to the "Who cares?" question. If you know that the particulars of your story contain the universal; if you trust that your story needs to be told and you need to tell it; if you have confidence enough to describe something as mundane as taking out the trash, then you must consider what it is about the chore that carries import. You have to find the mystery lurking beyond the self that is really the story's heartbeat. The question to ask in the midst of writing is: What is at stake?—not asked snidely or condescendingly, but with genuine curiosity. What is this anecdote trying to say? Why does it matter to you?

The "What is at stake?" question bridges the particular and the universal. By figuring out why I'm driven to write about garbage, I will find the element that touches a human chord. Perhaps the dirty task is actually valuable because it takes me outside into the evening hush and calms my mind. I discover a new meaning in trash as a lowest common denominator among people everywhere. This insight becomes an answer—not the answer, not even a complete answer, but still an answer to the question, What is at stake?

> ❧ *Answer the "What is at stake?" question for yourself in a journal entry. What will you get from the process of writing your story? Is this enough to make it worthwhile? Why or why not? If not, consider carefully the roles others play in satisfying your needs.*

Oddly enough, if you trust your impulse to write about garbage, digging around in the trash to discover what's in it for you, in this moment your reader is naturally drawn in. If you care enough, your care is persuasive. One of my favorite essays is called "What's Inside You, Brother?" by Touré, in which the author explores the blood-beating world of boxing. Touré is not very good at boxing but still finds himself compelled, time after time, into the ring. He writes to find out why. Now, I don't give a whit about this violent sport—and yet I'm hooked, not by the subject but by Touré's quest to uncover the appeal of boxing—his exploration of what's at stake. It turns out that as a black man, he feels he has taken too many punches sitting down. "I've got to fight, always fight, even in the face of sure defeat, because no one can hurt me as badly as I can," he writes.

Readers can only be engaged in a story as much as the author is engaged. In Touré's piece, he needs to get to the root of his reasons for boxing because his obsession frightens him; it's too dangerous to box when you're mediocre at it. There's a lot at stake for him emotionally and physically. As his reader, I feel the pressure of his subject—how boxing breaks through to the core of his personhood—and so I'm eager to trace his journey. Touré's story isn't about boxing after all; it's about peeling away layers of the psyche to find the underlying motivation for his actions. No wonder I'm drawn in. I'm curious about what instigates my own potentially self-destructive behavior, and I may find the answer by reading Touré.

> ❧ *What is the core question you're exploring in a piece of writing? Write it out. If this core question changes over time, revise it.*

Beginning writers often feel the instinct to leap forward to the reader's point of view and tailor the story to those ambiguous, projected expectations—not unlike high school students anticipating what the teacher wants to hear. They lean heavily on material they can address with authority, taking it for granted that their vast knowledge bolsters their right to take up printed space. Uncertainty is deemed weak and unappealing. In reality, the only stories *not* worth the reader's time are those that simply spout off the gleanings of experience with the purpose of enlightening the reader. Without a dose of humility and without continued openness to growth, writing swiftly becomes didactic and stale. There's nothing like an author's soapbox to make the reader feel condescended to and therefore uninterested.

Memoir writers must maintain a delicate balance between self-esteem and humility. The notion that your life story might be instructive to others is not a bad thing; without such audacious confidence you would never propel your thoughts on to the page. A certain conviction about your worth and the potential significance of your story places you in a broader conversation with society. Each of us has a right—even a responsibility—to give our story back to the community. If you have too little esteem for your story, you write nothing. Too much esteem can always be tempered in the humbling process of revision.

As with any spiritual discipline, writing places you squarely in an uncomfortable paradox. If you want your life's story to appeal to the reader, it must first appeal to you. When I begin to coach a writer through a memoir, I always ask, "What's in this project for you?" It's surprising how uncomfortable this question makes people feel. Yet, for the sake of the story, it's a question worth considering carefully, not only before you start but also throughout the process. What is at stake? Why do you care enough to devote hundreds of difficult hours for no pay? Why do you care for your own sake? The investment in discovering, learning, and growing through your writing reaps benefits in the reader's willingness to invest in your story. But the primary benefit is intrinsic to the process: You get to discover, learn, and grow. This, and not any rewards from the final product, keeps you motivated.

In the end, it takes a magnificent ego and vivacious humility to write memoir. You must assume that your story is of utmost value and be willing to find that value anywhere, even in the shadowed, dirty corners of self. You must plunge through resistance without knowing where you're going. You must, for a time, be content with only *you* as an audience. Since you have a choice, why not be inquisitive, probing, and compassionate?

Freedom on the Page

If you find yourself unable to write freely for fear of what others will think, try these exercises:

~ Write a memory that feels dangerous or threatening. Then burn your writing.

~ Store your writing in a lockbox.

~ Preface your writing with a note to snoopers. You can ask them not to read or to read with compassion for your point of view.

~ Make an agreement with someone you trust about what to do with your writing should you suddenly die or become incapacitated.

~ Share your writing with someone you have no history or emotional baggage with (not a friend or relative). Ask this person not to give you feedback but to simply hold your story. If you are comfortable, you might allow that person to ask questions or express appreciation. Practice living with the knowledge that someone else can hold your story.

These exercises teach that you control who sees your writing and when. Before your memoir reaches the press, years pass in which you hold the reigns of your readership. Take advantage of that freedom. Use it to write the truth. You can always make editorial choices that address the concerns of your audience later.

Another helpful exercise is to imagine a completely receptive, affirming reader. Create a character sketch of this person. Draw or describe his or her qualities in order to make them more present in your mind. How does this reader respond to your story? What connections do you and your reader share? Why is the reader so eager for your story? In her diary, Anne Frank writes to Kitty, her imaginary best friend. Kitty is infinitely curious about Anne's life and infinitely trustworthy. Some writers discover that their ideal reader is a real person and write their memoirs (at least the initial drafts) directly to that person. When you address a friendly audience, you are more apt to disclose difficult memories and ask taboo questions. Try to keep this audience in mind as you work.

Freedom to explore memories with integrity is more important than adherence to the facts. If fictionalizing others in your story (changing people's identity or conflating characters) allows you to write, by all means fictionalize. You can always wrestle with the dilemmas of truth versus fact when you revise. Initially, it's imperative that you simply begin.

Developing the Writing Habit

GETTING STARTED is difficult for beginning writers, but sustaining momentum through the long haul of creating even a short memoir can seem impossible. How swiftly we grow discouraged! How readily we discredit our work! The way to deal with these obstacles is to write a little every day. Fifteen minutes is doable and it makes a difference. Writing this much every day, regardless of what you write, sustains the habit.

If you are stalled, still honor your writing time. Do other things that nourish your writing: journal, read other memoirs, look through old photographs, draw pictures of memories. If you need to do research for your project, do it now. Dig around in your memory, interview family or friends, and visit places you're writing about. The writer inside will know you are staying faithful and will appear again eventually.

When you're stuck, write in your journal about being stuck. Have a conversation with your writer's block. Ask it questions, tell it your opinion, and engage it with writing.

Maintain equilibrium. Often beginning writers swing between two extremes: "This is crap!" at one end and "This is stunningly brilliant! I'll win the Pulitzer!" at the other. Chances are good neither is true. The majority of our writing resides somewhere in between—

sloppiness interrupted by periodic clarity, tired ideas littered with unconventionality. If you learn to have patience with yourself, you are more likely to recognize the gems buried in the slop. Maintaining balanced emotions in relation to writing helps you create realistic expectations, which in turn make writing sustainable.

Be clear about what is in the writing for you. Most writers peter out because their original motivation for writing is external. They write for someone else rather than themselves. Every time you put pen to page know what you stand to gain: Delight in language? A new discovery? The dynamic sensation of creation? The clarity of your own voice? A clearer understanding of your past? Even if the writing is painful, your certainty regarding its healing properties will sustain you through difficult passages. Remaining faithful to the story and to the creator within is itself a huge reward.

Bribery works. I know a writer who pays herself by the page. Treat yourself to a good cup of coffee after a successful writing session. My prize for a morning of sitting in front of the computer is a half hour of swimming laps.

Stop writing when the going's good. When I was in Girl Scouts, I learned a fabulous trick about playing games: Always stop while you're still having fun. If you keep playing Red Rover until you're sick of it, the game becomes tainted—not just in that instance but in the future as well. If you stop before then, you still like your playmates and you leave with fond recollections. The corollary in writing is to stop writing in the middle of a roll. That way you are eager to return to your project the next day. If you write your inspirations to the ground, you have to start from scratch every time. Try stopping midway through a sentence. That way you don't have to come up with a new thought to begin writing again.

Make notes about your ideas. Sometimes ideas come in torrents; there's no keeping up with them. At other times (most often inconvenient ones, such as in the middle of the night or in the shower), a single idea bubbles up. Sometimes at the end of a writing session you'll have a string of ideas that you know you want to follow. Whenever ideas emerge, write them down, regardless of what you're doing. I have written while I'm driving and have gotten out of the pool midway through laps in order to jot down a thought. Ideas are fleeting and precious.

Work on multiple projects. For some writers, the stimulation of a second project (or chapter within a project) helps fill the gaps when the first is stalled. Alternating between projects takes some coordination, but it can provide the distraction needed to gain energy for whatever lies fallow. The danger lies in beginning too many projects and never following one to completion.

Amass material. The primary work of a first draft is to generate material. Some of it will be good, but most of it will be quite rough. Don't get hung up on the quality of writing; that's the concern of revision. For now, quantity is enough.

The Dilemma of Memory

THE QUIRKINESS OF MEMORY first revealed itself to me in my freshman year of college. I was flabbergasted by the details in the books we read in memoir class—pages of dialogue, nuances of emotion, the repulsive shade of green on a grandfather's tic. "But we don't remember our past that clearly," the class complained, as though our childhoods resided centuries away. The professor explained that memory is a muscle and our memories were flabby. She started us on a rigorous workout of writing three pages of memories a day.

At first I paced the dorm room, uncertain what to write. A month later I was shocked by how many stories crammed my eighteen years. One crisp day as I shuffled through leaves on my walk across campus, flashbacks began to pile up in my brain. After years of disregarding my memory, the suddenly over-extended muscle was going into spasms. It was then that I knew the power of memory to be limitless. Access to that power becomes restricted with time if we don't tap it. Exercise strengthens the memory.

  Patricia Hampl writes, "How uncanny to go back in memory to a house from which time has stolen all the furniture, and to find the one remembered chair, and write it so large, so deep, that it furnishes the entire vacant room." Focus on one "piece of furniture" (in other words, a single object) that you considered holy or felt awe toward as a child. Describe it in detail. Then allow yourself to digress from this object into story or reflection in such a way that memory begins to "furnish the entire vacant room."

Memory is a mysterious faculty—one worth considering carefully if we intend to tap its resources for our writing. Consciously or unconsciously, we are remembering all the time. Every time we encounter grass in the spring, the 23 bus line, or Aunt Beulah's quilt, our response is shaped by every previous encounter. Memories build upon one another in layers.

Writing memoir needn't require living in the past. In fact, it's just the opposite: The present, with its unique questions and dilemmas, is the centerpiece of memoir. Personal history is pressing only when it is linked to a current state. I once worked with a writer who wrote reams of memories about his university years—the mischief, the dancing, the camaraderie. Underneath the jovial stories I sensed sadness. When I asked why these memories were so important, he responded, "Those were my best years."

"Can you explore that?" I pushed.

As he perceived it, his life had lost its social spark. It was his present sadness that made the happy times relevant. Without the context of his longing, the anecdotes were sentimental reminiscences that locked him in the past and left the reader wondering, "So what?"

Memoir is less about dwelling in the past and more about investigating the past for its impact on the present. In *The Woman Warrior*, Maxine Hong Kingston relates a story her mother told her about an aunt who committed suicide. Kingston's mother uses this tragedy to threaten the young girl into obedience. Years later Kingston is still haunted by her aunt's story. Alone, the story graphically exposes the moral constraints of Chinese village life and is a powerful historical anecdote. But it becomes memoir when Kingston traces her aunt's story into her own struggles living in America haunted by Chinese ghosts. "Unless I see her life branching into mine," Kingston writes, "she gives me no ancestral help." The branches of influence in memoir extend beyond any individual life into the realm of ancestors, national identity, cultural history, and a broad spiritual legacy.

Memoir straddles time. It finds the eternal within the particulars of an instant. Elie Wiesel, author of *Night* and holder of horrific memories from the Holocaust, writes that memory "is a passion no less powerful or pervasive than love. It is [the ability] to live in more than one world, to prevent the past from fading, and to call upon the future to illuminate it." Nuala O'Faolain puts it this way: "A memoir may always be retrospective, but the past is not where the action takes place." Memory is a window onto both the infinite and the particulars of the present moment.

If you understand *holiness* to be that which is worthy of regard, awe, and reverence, then certainly memories are holy. A fruitful question to ask as you're writing down bits from the past is, Why do I remember this? Chase down the mystery in any memory and you will encounter revelation. Memories carry some unknown factor, even when they appear utterly pedantic. I remember walking a basement corridor in high school and passing an open office door. The office was brightly lit, and in the two seconds it took for me to pass it, I caught a clear view of a secretary in mid-yawn. Her wide mouth and squeezed eyes were so striking, I thought to myself, "I will remember that for the rest of my life." On the surface, this is a whimsical memory. It makes me laugh to think of my teenage self sending a bizarre mental postcard to me today. But when I linger with the memory, when I take time to read that postcard, I know once again my young delight in ordinary surprises. I also see that extravagant yawn as a window into another life, a bored adult's life, and I have complete freedom to imagine the circumstances surrounding it. It's a mundane, quirky anecdote. But if I treat it with reverence, I find holiness in the clarity and humor and in my youthful conviction that the image was worth retaining.

The root word of religion is *religare*, which means "to bind back to the origin." While I'm reluctant to call memoir writing a religion, its movement is strikingly similar. To recognize Mystery, we must begin with the mysteries inherent to our own life. We must bind the present to the past and explore our own origins for insight into the universal origin.

> ᔕ *Write down a memory that you cherish. Reflect on how this memory continues to nourish you. When does the memory come to you? Why? What role does it play in your spiritual life?*

There is a common tendency to be embarrassed or ashamed by episodes in the past and, therefore, to avoid writing about them. Many of us have strong internal censors that filter ugly memories from public view and even from our own view. Sometimes these censors are useful. They protect us from memories we're not prepared to face or shelter us from the wrath of others. More often they are obsolete, inhibiting rather than safeguarding growth. By eliminating difficult memories from the story we tell ourselves about our lives, we create a pretty falsehood. Writing memoir requires a willingness to embrace our inadequacies. Gentleness and patience with ourselves are invaluable. In the battle between the drive to write and the discomfort with the past, you will find that reverence for the truth always holds you in good stead. Trust that truth—your truth—is always honorable, regardless of its content.

     ❧ *Choose a particularly difficult memory—one that you'd like to write about but find daunting or scary. Write about the memory with the third person point-of-view, using he or she instead of I. Return to the writing later and revise it into first person.*

Beware of the temptation to discuss the past in a demeaning way. For example, the poetry I wrote in junior high school was ghastly. I was in a period of high religious fervor; I filled pages of my journal with "Our Father" this and "Heavenly Creation" that. Describing my first efforts at verse, I am sorely tempted to belittle my twelve-year-old self. It's natural to want to make excuses for my concrete thinking and poke fun at the clichés I assumed I'd invented (and my affection for exclamation marks): "Life is a stage! I'm just an actor!" "Sunshine means so much more after rain!" Treating our young selves poorly—indeed, casting judgment on any former stage of our lives—only limits the story and distances the reader. Were I to judge those early poems offhand, I might not discover their sincerity or learn how they were the first containers for my initial awareness of God. Judgment would distance the reader, who may be thinking, "Ah, yes, I went through that stage too." Disrespect for myself swiftly becomes disrespect for my reader, thus increasing the chances that the reader will turn away. Better to heed Scott Russell Sanders' advice: "Don't condescend to your younger self. Your feelings back then have authority . . . Whatever you were as a child, you had a full heart."

Another common response to embarrassment is to deny or sugarcoat the past. Making the past appear better than it was corrodes the integrity of the story. Readers are supersensitive to authors' deceits, holding us to a high standard of honesty. I once worked with a writer on a healing memoir who had been ritually abused as a child and was eager to share his story of recovery. He described the scenes of confronting and forgiving his family. He told of solo trips in the north woods. He wrote about the men who performed rituals with him and formed his community. In the end, though, his book didn't work.

"You need to write about the abuse," I told him. "If your readers don't know the hurt, they are not going to understand the healing." In order for the healing to have relevance, the author had to disclose why healing was necessary. But he didn't want to delve into that messy, painful time. Understandably. Who would? Yet the author has a responsibility to the story itself, which always wants to keep its integrity. The story rebelled against the omission of the abuse; it refused to be a *whole* story unless its origins were told. It is impossible for a story with fundamental falsehoods to feel whole.

Instead of suffering the humiliation of your former self, imagine sitting at the feet of a younger you, probing him or her with questions. This younger you has a wisdom particular to an age and time, to which you no longer have access. That person is an expert on what age two or twelve or twenty-two is like; he or she intuits the healing power of play and temper tantrums and idleness and knows a sacred presence in stuffed bears, glasses of lemonade, and bare feet to a degree you have since forgotten. You can laugh at your younger self, be aware of his or her limitations, and wish the faults and circumstances were otherwise, but do not deny the truth of your younger self's experience.

෨ *Write a story about a childhood incident that you are not especially proud of. Practice showing compassion and patience with your younger self. What does the incident reveal about your weaknesses? How does it show your strengths? Reflect on both within the scene.*

As you write, you'll also find that certain memories wear out their welcome. How many times can you revisit your mother's death—in therapy, over coffee with friends, in your journal, and in memoir—without growing weary? When you have worked through a nagging issue and celebrated its resolution, the last thing you want is to face it again for yet another shade of awareness. And yet there are powerful events that refuse to leave us alone. A spiritual director once told me that she thinks of memory as a tall lighthouse with a spiral staircase climbing the inner chamber. The events of a life are narrow murals painted vertically on the inside walls. As we grow and change, we pass the same memories over and over. But each time we are higher up, viewing past events from a new perspective. The lighthouse image helps me to be patient with recurring memories. It also reminds me of the delights of rereading books—how *The Secret Garden*, a story I fell in love with as a child, is entirely different every time I read it because I have changed in the intervening years. Half of a memory's value resides in the lens of the present moment, which is always changing.

Memoirists often say that they remember things because they didn't learn all that the event had to teach the first time. Writing memoir helps memories disclose information and insights that are otherwise inaccessible. Louise deSalvo's *Writing as a Way of Healing* delves into the emotional, spiritual, and medically proven physical benefits of writing about the past. "To improve health," deSalvo writes, "we must write detailed accounts, linking feelings with events." We must describe both the feelings we experienced during the event and those we have in retrospect. Interestingly, deSalvo concludes that "the more writing succeeds as narrative—by being detailed, organized, compelling, vivid, lucid—the more health and emotional benefits are derived from writing." While writing is not a cure-all, it does help us find resolution and wholeness. Memoir holds the past, no matter how splintered and sharp. A ton of work is necessary to create the container that is memoir, and that work is done both within your being as well as on the page. Thus any fragment of memory has the potential to make a story whole.

Imagination

Memoir falls under the wide umbrella of creative nonfiction, a catch-all genre that includes personal essay, literary journalism, nature writing, and travel writing, among others. The term creative nonfiction is paradoxical; how can nonfiction be creative? It can, in two distinct ways: in its form and in its content. When we take the material of our lives and present it in a straightforward, logical manner, we write nonfiction. But when we play with the form, describing scenes in detail, using flashbacks and flash-forwards, developing our characters, and seeking out meaning, how we tell the story becomes just as important as what the story is about. Creativity sits on the same park bench with nonfiction.

> *Write a story that gets told about you, either by family or friends. What is your response to the "facts" of the story? How do*

you understand others' need to tell this story about you? How do you remember the event?

It is far more controversial when authors are creative with content. The term *nonfiction* sets up an expectation that the author is faithful to the truth. We cannot violate that implicit contract.

And yet truth is slippery, especially when working with memory. Try sharing your version of the worst family vacation ever with a sibling or parent. Invariably accusations of "That's not what happened!" are lobbed in your direction. In your account, the car was unbearably stuffy while you were driving across the desert. In your sister's account, the wind was ruining her Farrah Fawcett hairdo. Your dad, on the other hand, is certain you both slept the entire time. Even when you can agree on the details of what happened, the emotional impact of the memory remains unique for each person. How much of what you remember, then, is real? How much imagined?

The faculty of memory is far from reliable. First of all, we have a tendency to forget huge chunks of our history. My parents claim that when they packed my belongings into the station wagon and hauled me from New York to Minnesota to go to college, the family had the best trip ever. They reminisce about riding tandems on Mackinac Island and canoeing down the St. Croix River. I don't remember a lick of it, except for how we covered my guitar with a blanket and called it Aunt Tilly because it looked like a dead body lying under the back window. I'm sure I was panicked; I was leaving home for a college I'd never visited. My lack of memory becomes a story in itself. While my family rollicked across the country, I retreated into private anxiety, imagining my dorm room and unknown roommate rather than seeing Lake Michigan outside the car window. Shrouded Aunt Tilly now seems like a testimony to the death of my childhood.

    ↬ *Think of a moment in your past or in your family's past that contains more questions than answers. Explore it. Try writing several hypothetical explanations or scenarios of what happened. Reflect on why you may have forgotten certain parts of the story.*

What we do remember can often be terrifically inaccurate. Author Tony Earley recounts how, on July 20, 1969, he and his younger sister studied the moon through a surveyor's transit. "Peering through the eyepiece, I felt as if I could almost see Neil Armstrong on the lunar surface," he writes in *Somehow Form a Family*, calling the moment one of his most vivid memories. "When I wrote about that night almost thirty years later, I described the full moon in detail, how, once magnified, it had seemed almost too bright to look at." But then a fact-checker at *Harper's* magazine found out that the moon had been a waxing crescent that night. Earley refused to believe her. "When I looked it up for myself and discovered that she was right, I was faced on one hand with a memory so strong I was sure it had to be true, and on the other hand with an objective truth significantly different than what I remembered. At that moment I came to understand, if not embrace, the true nature of the phrase *creative nonfiction*." Memories are inherently faulty and biased, regardless of your commitment to recalling "what really happened."

    ↬ *Recall a significant conversation in your life (the first birds-and-bees lecture, a marriage proposal, the news of a loved one's death). Write it as dialogue—fast. Reflect on how much of the dialogue is memory and how much is invention.*

Not only are memories unreliable, but writing them down is fraught with hazards. Once the pen starts moving, the imagination has a tendency to take over. Suddenly the sunset you can barely remember blazes crimson, the confirmation conversation you had with your priest thirty years ago is a vivid dialogue, and you portray yourself in 1980 wearing designer jeans that, now that you think of it, you bought in 1983. Memory and imagination are twins. Each has its own personality, and yet they are eerily similar.

Often our first reaction to blatant digression from the facts is to censor ourselves. It's memoir, we reason; what we write should be true. Imagination is the evil twin, the tempter, goading us into exaggerations, conflations, and even downright lies. We assume that authenticity and honesty emerge when we adhere to what really happened, and that anything that digresses from fact violates our contract with the reader.

But the bloodline between memory and imagination is strong. Memory and imagination play tricks. They like to dress in each other's clothes. Both have stories to tell that are pressing and true. Toni Morrison, author of *Beloved* and *Song of Solomon*, writes almost exclusively fiction, yet she understands her drive to be that of a memoirist—to tell the emotional stories of her people, especially when she has only facts, as in slave narratives. In William Zinsser's anthology *Inventing the Truth*, Morrison explains the role of memory in fiction writing, revealing an instructive fluidity:

> No matter how "fictional" the account of these writers, or how much it was a product of invention, the act of imagination is bound up with memory. You know, they straightened out the Mississippi River in places, to make room for houses and livable acreage. Occasionally the river floods these places. "Floods" is

the word they use, but in fact it is not flooding; it is remembering. Remembering where it used to be. All water has a perfect memory and is forever trying to get back to where it was. Writers are like that: remembering where we were, what valley we ran through, what the banks were like, the light that was there and the route back to our original place. It is emotional memory—what the nerves and the skin remember as well as how it appeared. And a rush of imagination is our "flooding."

For Morrison, a rush of imagination is trustworthy. Imagination is a memory that, while perhaps not accurate in its facts, is reliable in describing emotional truth. As you write, consider spurts of questionable facts as memory flooding its banks. Floods are disruptive, but they fertilize the soil. Once they recede, it's worth looking carefully at what they left behind.

   Write the story of the day you were born. Make it as wild or realistic as you like, but be sure the details are in keeping with the truth of your entrance into the world. What happened? What didn't happen?

Memories invariably lead to invention. Even as you were learning to ride a bike or having a first mystical vision, you were inventing a story through which to understand the experience: "I'm a big boy now!" or "I must be crazy!" or "I've been chosen!" When you write these stories, even if you ruthlessly stick to the facts, you still invent context, interpretation, and emotional import. In other words, you invent the story's thrust. The imaginative parts of memoir are simply extensions of this inventive thrust. When you discover yourself inventing material in the effort to write memories, your inventions may disclose your real relationship to the memories, and are therefore worth heeding.

In her essay "Memory and Imagination" (a must-read for all fanciful memoirists), Patricia Hampl gives an example of an early draft of a memoir about her first piano lesson. Seven-year-old Hampl finds herself awed to be practicing beside Mary Katherine Reilly, whose grandfather invented the collapsible opera hat: "With the clairvoyance of all fated relationships based on dominance and submission, it was decided in advance: That when the time came for us to play duets, I should always play second piano, that I should spend my allowance to buy her the Twinkies she craved but was not allowed to have, that finally, I should let her copy from my test paper." Later Hampl confesses that in fact, she played first piano in their duets, never went to grade school with Mary Katherine, and certainly never let Mary copy her test papers as Mary was the better student. Why did these "lies" crop up in this early draft? Hampl reads them with an eye for their emotional content. "Why," she asks, "was I so impressed by that ancestral inventor of the collapsible opera hat? Did I feel I had nothing as remarkable in my own background?" Hampl's imaginative embellishments steer her to a more powerful truth—her ambivalence toward her father—that she pursues in the next draft. Like Hampl's fictive additions, those that appear in our own writing can be profoundly instructive. They show what's really at hand. They point to our story's emotional heart.

Whether or not our fictions remain in a story depends on our personal ethics and the purpose our fictions serve (for example, whether they make the story more accessible or protect the identity of others). Personal ethics vary widely. Carol Bly, author of *Beyond the Writer's*

Workshop, is adamantly opposed to toying with facts in nonfiction in any way, claiming it violates the writer–reader contract. I, on the other hand, am less certain that facts are inherently morally valuable. I have great respect for the facts, for things as they actually happened. But I'm unwilling to give them the final say-so. The underlying emotional truth is, for me, the ultimate authority.

This is not to say that the memoirist has creative license to rewrite the past. Inventing events that did not occur, denying events that did occur, altering emotional import, or constructing a story that misrepresents the complexity of lived experience are all profound violations of the story's integrity. The reader of memoir expects adherence to the truth. If you deviate widely from the truth, you betray the reader, who might then reject your story. It is wise then to either label your work as fiction or alert the reader to your fictions. Memoirists do the latter all the time with brief, unobtrusive signals: "I imagine," "perhaps," "It could have been that," "I wonder whether." The first chapter of *The Woman Warrior* is a prime example. Maxine Hong Kingston begins by sharing the few facts she has about her Chinese aunt who committed suicide. Once the reader knows all that Kingston knows, Kingston is free to speculate about the details of her aunt's life without fear of betraying the reader. And she does so with stunning intricacy: "Once my aunt found a freckle on her chin, at a spot that the almanac said predestined her for unhappiness." Because Kingston comes clean at the beginning, we're willing to ride her imagination into the details.

In "Under the Influence," Scott Russell Sanders takes another tack:

> After his final day of work . . . Father stayed behind to oversee the packing. When the van was loaded, the sweaty movers broke open a six-pack and offered him a beer.

"Let's drink to retirement!" they crowed. "Let's drink to freedom! To fishing! hunting! loafing! Let's drink to a guy who's going home!"

At least I imagine some such words, for that is all I can do, imagine, and I see Father's hand trembling in midair as he thinks about the fifteen sober years and about the doctor's warning, and he tells himself *God-damnit, I am a free man, and Why can't a free man drink after a lifetime of hard work?*

Inventions, which are a natural aspect of memory, needn't be erased from our stories. They influence us, regardless of their veracity. It is, however, a good policy to be honest about your dishonesty.

❧ *At the top of a blank page write the title "Lies about _____" and fill in the blank. Proceed, allowing yourself the freedom to write as many lies as you wish. Later, revisit them. In what ways do they reveal the truth? Incorporate what you've learned from the lies into a more factual account.*

Giving yourself some creative leeway in a story can make your experiences more accessible to your readers. Hampl's memoir *Virgin Time* is a good example. In reality, Hampl took two pilgrimages to Italy. But two similar journeys make a less shapely story than the smooth narrative arc of a single journey, so she conflates two into one. This allows the reader to explore prayer alongside the protagonist without confusion or boredom. I freely conflate the friends I write about, reducing two or three people into one, because it's too much to expect the reader to keep track of them all. I value my many friends as individuals, but in my writing I'm more interested in exploring the nature of friendship than each friend's particulars. I compromise the facts to serve a bigger purpose.

Conflation of characters also protects the identity of those I write about—a very practical reason to manipulate the facts. It's not uncommon for authors to disguise the people they write about so their neighbors don't discover their private foibles in the book. In some cases, writers put themselves in emotional, physical, or legal danger by writing honestly about others. A layer of fiction serves as protection for both the writer and the subject. Memoir writers commonly use pseudonyms. Our stories are intricately linked with others. It's important to respect people's privacy.

But not too much. Don't honor others at the expense of your own truth. I may make the kid who bullied me in junior high into a girl; I may give her baggy sweatpants and a gaggle of swaggering buddies. But the viciousness of the bully's words doesn't change, nor does my own hormonally charged hatred. Portraying anyone with false kindness does a disservice to the story, yourself, your reader, and even to the person you're describing. People are complex—faulty, bright, hurtful, and hurting. We honor them best by not denying their many faces.

Ultimately it is impossible to render lived experience accurately and objectively on the page. As soon as you choose where to begin, you have truncated reality in order to fit a frame. "When we articulate our lives," writes Karen Brennan, "we are already in the arena of fiction— the self of the past being essentially unrecoverable." Thus, the imagination plays a vital role in the writing of memoir and ought not to be so badly maligned. If you're still tempted to stick to "just the facts," consider Carl Jung's words in *Memories, Dreams, Reflections*:

> Imagination is an authentic accomplishment of thought or reflection that does not spin aimless and groundless fantasies

into the blue; that is to say, it does not merely play with its object, rather it tries to grasp the inner facts and portray them in images true to their nature. This activity is an opus, a work. Imagination is essential to the creation of your own opus.

Faith

The developmental psychologist James Fowler understands faith to be an imaginative function. In his book *Stages of Faith* he carefully distinguishes faith from belief. Faith, he writes, is a way of seeing everyday life in relation to whatever we perceive is the ultimate value or power. By this definition, faith is a universal human attribute. Everyone has an "alignment of the will, a resting of the heart, in accordance with . . . one's ultimate concern." Faith steers our thoughts and actions, often without our direct awareness. Belief, on the other hand, is an effort to translate faith into concepts or propositions. Belief systems—religion and tradition—are means of making faith visible, graspable, and manageable.

Writing our spiritual stories often exposes incongruity between belief and faith. For three years I taught seventh grade in a wealthy, conservative suburb of Minneapolis. Every morning I rose at five-thirty, wrote from six to six-thirty, and then drove to Minnetonka to face 130 twelve- and thirteen-year-olds. I'd taken up teaching because it was responsible, worthy work, and I felt an obligation to return to the world the care I'd been given by my own teachers. During this period, my understanding of the sacred was shifting due to the impact of feminine images of God. Had you asked what my credo was, I would have answered, "I am made in God's image." I was also growing aware of my bisexual identity and becoming increasingly aware of the hazards of being "deviant" in the suburbs. I denied the sacred worth of my body, even pretended it didn't exist, and I constricted my impulse to write because it seemed irresponsible. Eventually I confronted a shocking truth: What I believed and how I oriented my life—my work, time, energy, and money—were two separate things. I may have *believed* in a creative, creating God, but I placed my *faith* in security and being responsible to society. Belief can be an extension of faith, but it can also exist in our heads and our verbalized convictions, quite separate from the true alignment of our hearts.

This distinction between articulated belief and lived faith is extremely helpful to the spiritual writer. While the content of belief is rich and worth exploring, it is faith—according to Fowler, the "orientation of the total person, giving purpose and goal to one's hopes and strivings, thoughts and actions"—that comes to light in our stories.

     Reflect on a discrepancy between what you believe and how you live. Without judgment, write what it feels like to live with this dichotomy. What role does this tension play in your soul's journey?

Fowler says that our response to a transcendent value or power is essentially imaginative. He looks to the Hindi term for faith, sraddha, to trace the connection. Sraddha means "to set one's heart on." To set one's heart on something involves vision and commitment. If your heart is set on wealth, you imagine the possibilities of riches and commit yourself to achieving a mansion and flashy car. If your heart is set on selflessness, you create a vision of simplicity and commit yourself to letting go of possessions and attachments. In either case, you would use your imagination to bring about your goal. Both are acts of faith.

At its core, all creative writing requires an imaginative leap. How much more so when we use writing to explore faith! As a teenager sitting by the Hudson River, I sensed a unitive potential in myself, in the river, in all of creation. That imagined possibility infused me with longing and drove me to write. Emily Bronte demonstrates the power of imagination to influence change when she writes, "I've dreamt in my life dreams that have stayed with me ever after, and changed my ideas: they've gone through and through me, like wine through water, and altered the color of my mind." When we use writing to explore imagination, our faith is launched into a realm of real consequence.

Fowler also examines a German term for imagination, *einbildungskraft*, "literally, the 'power (*kraft*)' of 'forming (*bildung*)' into 'one (*ein*).'" What else are we doing when writing spiritual memoir but forming a unified portrait of the spiritual journey? From a purely secular point of view, Carol Bly writes, "Feeling that life is meaningful is oddly related to having a developed imagination. If you can see in your mind one thing that your eyes have never seen, you can give design to your own life." To take the messy material of life and give it design, cohesion, and unity requires imagination and faith. Without proof, we must trust that "the interior life is a real life, and the intangible dreams of people have a tangible effect on the world," as James Baldwin writes. As an author you must trust that your story makes a difference.

And so the memoir we so innocently embarked on swiftly becomes a test of faith. No wonder spiritual memoir writing can seem overwhelming and all-consuming. Memory is more slippery than we thought, imagination more trustworthy, and faith and belief are a muddle of mystery. From this confusion, our memoirs ask that we move forward anyhow, staking our faith in the story's integrity.

Organizing Your Memories

WHILE YOUR FIRST JOB in writing a memoir is to simply generate material, it's often a relief when an organizational structure guides your first draft and adds some order to the chaos. The following techniques will help you organize your vast resource of memories and provide greater perspective on your work.

Draw a map of your spiritual journey. Through what territory has your spirit traveled? What are the landmarks, the turning points, the difficult terrain, the resting places? What are the stepping stones, bridges, wildernesses, oases, and mountain peaks? Designate these landmarks on a large piece of paper using simple drawings, words, or pictures clipped from magazines. Be sure to mark moments of great realization, extreme doubt, despair, etc. Then make note of any significant memories that are attached to these landmarks. This map provides a bird's-eye view of your story—a way to see the whole at a glance. What aspect of the map intrigues or surprises you? Perhaps that is where you can begin writing.

Create a time line. If you are a linear thinker, a time line of your life serves the same purpose as a map but gives it a linear structure. Be sure to include the dates of both external and internal events.

Cluster your memories. Clustering, or mind mapping, is a marvelous brainstorming technique. In the center of a large piece of paper, write a topic that intrigues you (a memory, theme, or question) and draw a circle around it. Then, in lines spidering from that center, write down all that you associate with that topic. Include memories, sayings, questions, dreams, anecdotes, and whatever else occurs to you. If any of these items conjure up new ideas, trace these thoughts outward as well until you've created a network of topics. Clustering allows you to represent your mind's associative leaps quickly and easily. When you're done clustering, ask yourself which branches surprise you or carry energy. These are good places to begin writing.

Create chunks of writing around a single question. This technique is used by essayists, but it works equally well for memoirists. If you have many disparate memories that don't yet connect in your mind, give yourself permission to develop them as independent chunks of writing. Small bits always feel more manageable. When Scott Russell Sanders was exploring his father's alcoholism, he wrote dozens of chunks: memories of his father buying wine at the local grocery, lists of words people use to describe drunks, stories from television and the Bible that informed his thinking about alcohol, descriptions of his own addiction to work, and more. Sanders developed each chunk on its own before worrying about how they all fit together. Sometimes you have to allow fragments of material to grow before you can see a pattern. Eventually you cut some chunks, tighten others, and expand on others. But you don't know what will work until the material is on the page. It's like creating a collage; you cut out many small images and spread them on the table before choosing a few to compose a larger image.

YOUR SPIRITUAL LIFE
AS SUBJECT MATTER

Maybe then the problem of identifying the spiritual is simply a subtle one requiring a sharp eye and a talent for reading the resonance of events. To perceive the spiritual in a slice of life or a piece of art we may have to make a good story of it, because a story has the uncanny ability to raise the spirit out of the flesh like bread rising yeasty in a warm place.

—THOMAS MOORE

Describing the Indescribable

I REMEMBER THE FIRST TIME I showed the manuscript of my spiritual memoir to Mary Rockcastle, a Minnesota novelist and mentor of mine. She circled my every use of the word *God*, *Spirit*, or *Sacred* and wrote in the margins, "What do you *mean*?" It made me furious! I wanted to flap the pages in her face and shout, "Isn't it obvious?" But the more I thought about it, the more I realized it wasn't at all obvious. *God* meant something entirely different to me at age twenty-five (a companionable presence, inviting me into my fullest self) than it did at age five (a mother's love) or at age thirteen (a bearded white man in the sky). When I say the word *God* it is infused with my unique experiences, the teachings of my religious tradition, and many mysteries I can't yet articulate. When I say God I mean something quite different from what a fundamentalist Christian might mean, or a Jew, or indeed any other individual. I can make no assumptions that the reader will know what I mean.

Perhaps the greatest challenge in writing about the spiritual life is how to keep language precise. Those of us brought up in strong religious traditions inherit a linguistic blessing alongside a curse. Sacred texts, with their beloved lyricism, narrative drive, candle-lit imagery, and histories of discourse, bestow a literary heritage; we can be inspired by our traditions and place our own writing in the context of this larger continuity. When I explore my breath as a manifestation of divinity, my words resonate with the Christian creation story, God breathing life through Adam's nostrils, and with *Ruah*, the Hebrew spirit creating life out of chaos and liberation out of slavery, and with Spirit—*spiritus*, Latin for *breath*. I am formed by my traditions; I cannot escape how it layers my words.

Tradition is a dangerous gift, however, because it's easy to take religious words for granted. Even if you aren't heavily influenced by a religious tradition, it is difficult not to be affected by the secularized version of Christianity that underpins our culture. Everyone is susceptible to the language ruts of religion.

God bless you; Jesus saves; one day at a time; good karma, bad karma; be present in the moment: Most explanations of faith rely on clichés that, with overuse and lack of critical reflection, have lost their juiciness as well as their capacity to accurately portray reality. After all, what does it mean to "give yourself to Jesus"? Patricia Hampl calls this the "eau-de-cologne language of spirituality." It's sickly sweet, cheap, and easy to spout. If we use modern literary standards to sort through the high volume of prayer, profession, liturgy, and doctrine that comprise much of religious tradition, we will need to toss huge boxes of words out the window. What's left is ambrosia on the tongue and sustenance for our souls.

Good writers don't walk in language ruts, no matter how faithful they are to their tradition. They constantly seek out fresh means for touching the essence of the human condition and their own personal truth. The best response to the stories of our faith is to create new stories—our own stories. The best language for discussing sacred ✓ experience is not that of the church, synagogue, mosque, or coven; nor is it the theologian's, psalmist's, or Zen master's language. It's our own.

> ❧ *Choose a cliché from your spiritual tradition that you use frequently. Using your own natural, internal language—your slang and quirky expressions, your most casual voice—rewrite the cliché to illustrate the meaning it holds for you.*

Language ruts are a symptom of a larger language dilemma that affects spiritual memoir: *Spirituality*, by definition, is the dimension of our being that relates to the inexplicable. When we ponder the infinite, say the rosary, follow our breath into silence, feel gratitude, speak with veracity, create art, or participate in any transformative activity, we put ourselves in dynamic relationship with . . . what? Meaning? Truth? Love? These words are paltry. Spirituality addresses the unknown, and it's impossible to write about what we do not know. Thus spiritual writers inhabit an uncomfortable paradox: We must describe the indescribable; we must use words, those inadequate cages, to hold an airy and indomitable bird.

The dictionary calls the *spiritual* "not tangible or material." Any writer worth his or her salt knows that if images and language are not tangible, the writing isn't spiritual: it is a flop. Grand abstractions (such as *soul, God, truth*) give the impression of being spiritual but are in fact vague and slippery. You can say, "God is love" and in the name of God murder abortion clinic physicians. Or you can say, "I passed a stranger on my walk yesterday. She looked me directly in the eyes, which is unusual in the city, and a grin spread across her tanned face. I welled up as though I'd swallowed sunshine, and I smiled back. That felt like

God." The spiritual may be not tangible, but spiritual writing, if it intends to move readers' hearts, demands the tangible, the concrete, the material. What a conundrum! The commonplace—a steaming cup of tea, a newspaper picked up by the wind, a scarred and callused hand—has the capacity to encompass ultimate mystery. If we want to convey the sacred, we must welcome the ordinary into our writing.

> ❧ *Create a list of names for the sacred, particularly those taught by your tradition. Then create a list of images of the sacred from your life. Note how the personal images create an emotional reaction and a visual picture, while the abstractions remain vague, heady concepts.*

One of the best examples of a writer facing the indescribable with both bafflement and linguistic fortitude is a passage from Peter Matthiessen's *The Snow Leopard*:

> I chanted the Kannon Sutra with such fury that I "lost" myself, forgot the self—the purpose of the sutra, which is chanted in Japanese, over and over, with mounting intensity. At the end, the Sangha gives a mighty shout that corresponds to OM!—this followed instantly by sudden silence, as if the universe had stopped to listen. And on that morning, in the near darkness—the altar candle was the only light in the long room—in the dead hush, like the hush in these snow mountains, the silence swelled with the intake of my breath into a Presence of vast benevolence of which I was a part: in my journal for that day, seeking in vain to find words for what had happened, I called it the "Smile." The Smile seemed to

grow out of me, filling all space above and behind like a huge shadow of my own Buddha form, which was minuscule now and without weight, borne up on the upraised palm of this Buddha-Being, this eternal amplification of myself. For it was I who smiled; the Smile was Me. I did not breathe, I did not need to look; for It was Everywhere. Nor was there terror in my awe: I felt "good," like a "good child," entirely safe. Wounds, ragged edges, hollow places were all gone, all had been healed; my heart lay at the heart of all Creation. Then I let my breath go, and gave myself up to delighted immersion in this Presence, to a peaceful belonging so overwhelming that tears of relief poured from my eyes, so overwhelming that even now, struggling to find a better term than "Smile" or "Presence," the memory affects me as I write. For the first time since unremembered childhood, I was not alone; there was no separate "I."

We can feel Matthiessen straining to write about this moment. He works with abstractions (vast benevolence, Buddha-Being, eternal amplification) and concrete images (the candle, the smile, his breath). He shares his frustration that he finds the words wanting. He is also forthcoming about the continued emotional impact of the memory. Matthiessen's helplessness in the face of his experience, combined with grounding details, links the awesome to the ordinary, making it available to the reader.

Thus the language of spiritual memoir requires movement into story. People read memoir to discover the grit of an author's life—how an evangelical upbringing spurs a lifelong passion for music, how handling snakes in Appalachia induces ecstasy, what it means to attend a Zen-center budget meeting with "no self." Memoir demands story. And story requires detail so that the reader can walk around in the author's unique shoes.

When the spiritual writer uses specific details, professed beliefs sometimes reveal themselves to be incongruent with our experience. I might say "God is love," but as soon as I write about running from committee meeting to committee meeting until I'm ragged and about my guilt for not volunteering at the food shelf, I recognize that I am responding to a God of judgment, not a God of love. This is why I relish the memoirs of spiritual gurus. Their inspirational writing may be profound, but their memoirs hold every spiritual vagary accountable to the hard details of life. Abstractions can lie; specifics can't. Any gaps between what you profess to believe and how you behave are exposed in memoir. Details always reveal the deeper story.

The challenge of finding precise, energetic language for your spiritual journey is really an advantage. Rather than striving for large words and sweeping ideas, enter the realm of memory. It contains all the details and images you need to illustrate the spiritual life. Not only that, but your memory is a lens on the sacred that is matchless and undeniable. If you avoid abstractions and the language ruts of tradition, if you move away from what you think you believe and instead describe your bare experiences, you arrive at your singular story and its consecrated contribution to the world.

The Power of Epiphany

THE FIRST TIME I heard the word *epiphany* was in church. *Epiphany* was a revered, extraordinary word like *Pentecost* and *Advent* and *Maundy Thursday*, and came as one of Christmas's mild aftershocks, when the wise men arrived and we kids got to carry pretend gold, incense, and myrrh down the center aisle to the altar. The congregation sang "We Three Kings," even though department stores had stopped playing that song on December twenty-fifth. The pastor preached about following your star.

I didn't encounter the word *epiphany* outside of church until my senior year of high school. Dr. Jim Quinn, a short, bouncy man with an impressive collection of plaid suit jackets, was my English teacher. He taught James Joyce, Yeats, Lord Dunsany, and Seamus Heany, thereby sending into the world generations of college-bound kids who revered Irish writers above all others. Researching my senior thesis on *Portrait of the Artist as a Young Man* by James Joyce, I encountered the word *epiphany* describing Stephen Dedalus's transformation on the beach after a young woman looks at him: "Her eyes had called him and his soul had leaped at the call. To live, to err, to fall, to triumph, to recreate life out of life!" The reference books define *epiphany* as a sudden, transformative revelation. Then I uncovered the definition by James Joyce himself, "when something's soul, its whatness leaps to us from the vestment of its appearance." How wonderful! Even more wonderful that I knew exactly what he meant. I daresay my discovery of the word *epiphany* was an epiphany itself.

> ✑ *Recall an ecstatic experience. When did the soul of something leap up to touch your own? Linger with the description of that indescribable moment. Use all your senses; describe what was happening in your body as well as your spirit.*

The word *epiphany* joins two worlds: the spiritual and the literary. The moment when Christ appears to the Magi widens to include any divine manifestation and then widens further to include the revelation of anything's essential, awesome nature. Epiphanal moments are instances of numinosity, when a veil is dropped from our eyes and we know the world for what it is, rough-hewn and sparkling. Epiphanies stand out as touchstones, bright instances among vague memories that we can latch on to and write from. Inherent in epiphanies are movement and growth—the elements necessary to make any story gripping. When we work with our epiphanies, we encounter mystery.

Because of this, epiphanal moments are a great place to begin writing. They are rich, sensory memories when time appears to slow down, and so we can linger in our writing, relishing the details. Nuances of internal transformation are so slight, so hard to identify, that they force us to look outward for concrete images on which to hang our words. When we explore moments of radical change, we're really asking, What went on here? Mystery is exactly what epiphanies invite us to explore— binding our marrow and sinew to the ineffable realm of change.

❧ Childhood epiphanies are a great place to start writing because the intervening years provide perspective. Recall an epiphanal moment from your childhood. Perhaps you realized something was beautiful, came into a sudden consciousness (I remember the first time I realized that I was thinking!), or you learned some terrible truth (about death, about Santa Claus, about your family). Perhaps you had a religious awakening. Write the story of your epiphany.

Not all epiphanies are as ecstatic as Stephen Dedalus's. I remember the moment I thought I had discovered corruption. It was during the science fair in my junior year of high school. One of my friends had stolen another friend's data. Of course I hoped the deception would be obvious to the judges, who would then set things right by awarding the original research. I sat in the floppy, fold-down seat of the auditorium eager for the final envelope to be opened. But after the drumroll, the name they read was the wrong one. I burst into tears. The judges had been persuaded by my gregarious, manipulative white friend. She would be the one to represent the school nationally in Hawaii. The real scientist, unrecognized, a shy girl from Taiwan, would continue her petri dish experiments in Yonkers, New York, because she cared about the results. I felt betrayed by my cheating friend, stunned that the judges hadn't seen through her, and furious that such injustice could go unchecked. Afterward I cried for four hours straight. The harder I cried, the more I knew I was grieving not just this petty high school drama but the corruption and racial discrimination that were inherent to adulthood. I had hoped to leave unfairness behind with social cliques and snobbery about clothes. The night of the science fair, I cried myself into a more accurate portrayal of the world I'd inherited. The "whatness" that leapt to me was bitter.

Not all epiphanies are of life-changing proportions. A simple, well-placed newspaper article or three-pronged, maple-seed helicopter can wake us up to the world in minute but invaluable ways. These instances are also worth writing about. They are the incremental steps that accumulate to create spiritual movement. They count.

> ✍ *Write a seemingly shallow epiphany in detail (such as when you realized another person disliked you or when you ate liver for the first time). Describe your internal transformation, however minute.*

To learn how epiphanies work in spiritual memoir, let's consider again *The Confessions of St. Augustine*. Augustine lived licentiously, had a child out of wedlock, and participated in a sect that spurned Christianity. In his early thirties, when he was sitting in a garden with his friend, a raw opening of his heart led to his conversion. This conversion became the centerpiece of his autobiography. His story is divided into *before* and *after* this moment in the garden. He portrays his life before as sinful and evil, and afterward as blessed by God. Augustine's conversion is a transformative event unequaled by any other in his life:

> But when deep reflection had dredged out of the secret recesses of my soul all my misery and heaped it up in full view of my heart, there arose a mighty storm, bringing with it a mighty downpour of tears. That I might pour it all forth with its own proper sounds, I arose from Alypius's side—to be

alone seemed more proper to this ordeal of weeping—and went farther apart, so that not even his presence would be a hindrance to me. . . . I flung myself down, how I do not know, under a certain fig tree, and gave free rein to my tears. The floods burst from my eyes, an acceptable sacrifice to you. Not indeed in these very words but to this effect I spoke many things to you: "And you, O Lord, how long? How long, O Lord, will you be angry forever? Remember not our past iniquities." For I felt that I was held by them, and I gasped forth these mournful words, "How long, how long? Tomorrow and tomorrow? Why not now? Why not in this very hour an end to my uncleanness?"

Such words I spoke, and with most bitter contrition I wept within my heart. And lo, I heard from a nearby house, a voice like that of a boy or a girl, I know not which, chanting and repeating over and over, "Take up and read. Take up and read." Instantly, with altered countenance, I began to think most intently whether children made use of any such chant in some kind of game, but I could not recall hearing it anywhere. I checked the flow of my tears and got up, for I interpreted this solely as a command given to me by God to open the book and read the first chapter I should come upon. . . .

So I hurried back to the spot where Alypius was sitting, for I had put there the volume of the apostle when I got up and left him. I snatched it up, opened it, and read in silence the chapter on which my eyes first fell: "Not in rioting and drunkenness, not in chambering and impurities, not in strife and envying; but put you on the Lord Jesus Christ, and make not provision for the flesh in its concupiscences." No further wished I to read, nor was there need to do so. Instantly, in truth, at the end of this sentence, as if before a peaceful light streaming into my heart, all the dark shadows of doubt fled away.

Thus the conversion narrative was born. The story pivots around a single, consummate epiphany. Christian writing is rife with conversion narratives, although the form appears in other religious traditions as well (*The Autobiography of Malcolm X* being a notable one).

Epiphanies of conversion proportions are fairly rare. More often epiphanies come in small doses that accumulate over time. Most of us stumble along overgrown spiritual paths and only rarely glimpse the vistas before and behind us. Still, it is helpful to look at extremes like Augustine's epiphany because they teach us how to write epiphanies. To understand the full impact of Augustine's conversion readers first need a thorough picture of his irreverence and illicit behavior. The worse we understand Augustine's behavior to be, the more dramatic his change. This means that a great deal of an epiphany's story occurs prior to the actual experience.

> ❧ *Small and large epiphanies continue to open our eyes throughout adulthood. Write the story of an epiphany that evolved slowly, one that shifted you in some fundamental manner. What's different now?*

When exploring epiphanies it is helpful to ask, Who was I before? In the story of the science fair fiasco I was a teenager who had hoped—perhaps even believed—that adults would be more just than my backbiting peers and that integrity and hard work would be rewarded.

Without my idealism the judges' decision would have been less shocking. Who was I afterward? A high school student who knew that adults don't always serve up justice. The epiphany moved me from a place of innocence to one more prepared for adult realities. So then, what happened internally and externally to make this change? The challenge is to articulate the many dynamics that comprise transformation so that the reader not only follows the story but also, in the best of circumstances, experiences the epiphany for him- or herself. Ultimately this is the gift of a well-written epiphany: What was transformed in the writer is transformed in the reader, who looks up from the page into a more brilliant and biting world.

Symbols and Metaphors

SHORTLY AFTER HIS PARTNER Wally died of AIDS, Mark Doty, the author of *Heaven's Coast*, took a series of walks at Hatch's Harbor on Cape Cod. Five times he saw seals there, surfacing in the waves, wounded on the sand, beached and dying, decaying, and finally, peering at him from the ocean. The otherworldly nature of the seals led Doty to reflect on his loss and what it meant that Wally's spirit no longer resided in his body. The seals seemed to be intermediaries between this world and the next. Doty writes,

> I am filled, entirely, with the image of my wounded lover leaping from his body, blossoming into some welcoming, other realm. Is it that I am in that porous state of grief, a heated psychic condition in which everything becomes metaphor? Or does the world consent, in some fashion, to offer me the particular image which imagination requires?

The seals confront Doty repeatedly with the bare fact of the body's death and of a watery, otherworldly presence.

Whether his grief gives him an open heart or the world itself is generous in its images, Doty demonstrates that the job of the spiritual memoirist is to read the world like a book. Medieval monks believed the natural world was a scriptural text, *liber mundi*, requiring as much study and devotion as the Bible. This impulse is literary as well: Writers are constantly alert to the environment, seeking out its inherent metaphoric resonance. Take, for example, this passage from May Sarton's *Journal of a Solitude*:

> Lately a small tabby cat has come every day and stared at me with a strange, intense look. Of course I put food out, night and morning. She is so terrified that she runs away at once when I open the door, but she comes back to eat ravenously as soon as I disappear. Yet her hunger is clearly not only for food. I long to take her in my arms and hear her purr with relief at finding shelter. Will she ever become tame enough for that, to give in to what she longs to have? It is such an intense look with which she scans my face at the door before she runs away. It is not a pleading look, simply a huge question: "Can I trust?" Our two gazes hang on its taut thread. I find it painful.

Sarton spent a year alone in her New Hampshire home observing the seasons, her neighbors, and her home, constantly reading the external world for evidence of her internal world. "When I talk about solitude I am really talking also about making space for that intense, hungry face at the window, starved cat, starved person. It is making space to *be there*," she writes. She recognizes her own needs in the stray cat's eyes and the challenge of solitude as meeting whatever arrives with a willing heart. Rather than accepting the hungry stray at face value, Sarton asks what the cat's presence has to say about her own solitude and about the nature of solitude in general.

The practice of reading the world is basic to creative writing. So much of art depends on the attention and perception of the artist—qualities that exist long before the creative process begins. Writers must become increasingly attuned to our surroundings, taking in through every sense the events, people, and places that compose our universe. And we must be ever more observant of our interior—the slow, shifting self; the well of emotions; the body; and the unconscious labyrinth linking individual to humanity. The marriage of exterior and interior, of image and its import, births the soul of our stories.

> ❧ *Choose a small part of your home (a corner, a window, a wall) and describe it in detail. What fills this space? How? What are your emotional responses to it? After creating a clear picture and reflecting on your relationship to the space, ask yourself, "How does this external space reflect my internal space?"*

It's not as though every object or creature has some hidden meaning that you must decipher. This kind of literal reading of the world becomes constraining and laborious. It reminds me of studying poetry in high school. Our concretely thinking minds understood metaphor as a code, each symbol corresponding to some secret meaning. When a river image appeared in a poem, we students overlooked our own knowledge of the Hudson and tried to guess the author's devious intent.

Poetic images are not so simplistic, and the multifaceted, largely uncommunicative world cannot be codified that easily. The seals on the beach meant something entirely different to the next passerby who followed Doty. During a different year, a hungry cat might remind Sarton of the tension between her domesticity and her ache for freedom. Likewise, the import of potent religious symbols is highly relative and difficult to pin down. The Eucharist's meaning shifts slightly with every communion service I attend. I value it for reasons quite different from those of my kneeling neighbor or the newly converted Catholic in Los Angeles or the evangelical missionary in Ethiopia.

When the import of any symbol gets locked down, it loses its vitality and potential for good. The linguist Owen Barfield goes so far as to say, "All literalism is idolatry." How this quote applies to faith is the work of scholars, but how it applies to writing is relevant to every person striving to pen a story. When I was in grade school, I had a recurring nightmare in which I'd miss the school bus and have to walk two miles to school. In my most memorable version of this dream, the streets were flooded after a hurricane. I swam to school holding my pencils and notebook in the air with one hand so they wouldn't get wet and I'd be able to write. I could say with some conviction that this dream image represents how writing was a lifeline for me from an early age. But the dream sticks with me; it is multidimensional. Getting to school was important to me—school was where I developed my independence and where I learned—but I had to work hard to hang on to the private, fanciful world I accessed through writing. Holding both priorities made mundane activities like getting myself to school quite difficult. I read all this in my dream and am still unwilling to say I understand the dream entirely. So long as the dream's meaning remains open, it continues to speak to me. Once I definitively lock down an interpretation, the dream ceases to reveal itself.

    Consider an image from your religious tradition, a memory, or a dream for which you have a standard interpretation. Revisit the image, opening to the possibility that it may contain

other layers of meaning. Begin by simply describing the image,
then move slowly into reflection.

Like dream images, sensory experiences—the fan whirling over-
head, the wilting vase of coneflowers, the glass of iced tea sweating a
pool on the desk—are expansive and inexhaustible in their associations. Thomas Moore calls this the "poetics of everyday life." We must
read images lightly, loosely, without judgment or ulterior motive. An
open heart makes space for images to share the fullness of their presence rather than a single, obvious dimension. At the same time, each
image has inherent qualities that distinguish it from every other
image. A swimming seal will always embody sleek, watery freedom; a
hungry stray will always represent wild neediness. Pen and paper
inevitably evoke writing. The Eucharist, for all its contemporary inter-
pretations as the bread of life and cup of compassion, will always
retain its Christian origin in a meal prior to a brutal loss and an inexplicable resurrection.

A literal reading of an image is idolatrous only if the figurative
qualities are denied. For instance, I just got back a roll of film that
includes a delightful photograph of my sister and me playing Russian
Bank, our favorite card game. We're highly competitive and prone to
calling each other nasty names and sticking our tongues out at each
other. In the photograph the playing cards are spread on a round table.
I sit with my back to the camera but you can see my arms folded across
my chest, a smirk on my face, and my back stretched as though to
make me look taller. Marcy, across the table, is hunched over with an
impish grin. Certainly she's got something naughty planned. To read
this image only literally as two sisters playing a game is limiting; such

simplicity denies the photo's wisdom. Yes, we're playing, but I'm the big sister clinging to my authority with my body (most likely I'm losing) while Marcy relishes her role as young mischief-maker. There's an invisible cord connecting my stand-offish posture to Marcy's eagerness; in a manner, our entire relationship can be understood in that dynamic connection. The love bond between us is strong enough to push and pull, to work out our sense of self against each other. When I read this image both literally and figuratively, its soul seeps through.

Your work as a writer is to listen to the "whatness" of creation—its essence, its speech—and discover where your own "whatness" leaps to meet it.

     Describe in detail the items in your coat pocket or pocketbook. What meaning have you already given them? What else might they symbolize about you or about your life?

One day recently I took my afternoon swim at a local college. As I was doing the breaststroke, it suddenly occurred to me that as an adult I've come to understand water's presence in my life as sacred—how it buoys me, is both willful and fluid and composes my very being. I had never considered this in connection with my childhood dream of swimming to school. In this light, I might understand the dream hurricane that hindered my trip to school to be holiness disrupting and saturating my childhood. To this day, I'm floundering through the flood with pen and paper in hand, trying to read the book of the world.

The Vividness of Childhood

THE UNIFYING PRINCIPLE of spiritual memoir is most often an aspect of the author's adult spiritual life, but invariably childhood—with its spontaneous, unadulterated encounters with mystery—squirms its way into our writing. Beware of resisting it. Those earliest memories are feisty and can flatten any exploration of adult memories if suppressed. Besides, our best writing often emerges from memories of childhood, when every moment was unexpected and sharp. Back then we met the world in our bodies, taking in directly its sensory overtures. Only later, in early adolescence, did we learn to filter experiences through the screen of language. When the congregation of my childhood church prayed in unison, I heard the merging intonations, breaths, and conviction long before I understood the meaning. My earliest sense of a sacred presence came through my parents, but after that it was Teddy, his head resewn tightly to his torso, and my blue blanket with its silky hem that brought me companionship and tangible comfort (at least until laundry day). Visceral first memories are an excellent place to begin writing because they force touch, sight, smell, taste, and sound into the foreground. Suddenly we're shorter than the dining room table and fascinated by the scab on our knee. Our emotions are fierce and pure.

Just as some parents may witness their kids digging in the dirt or furiously dancing in the living room and recognize their future careers, writing our primary experiences can shed light on the nature of our souls. At the root of every spiritual passion lie our first passions, as simple and childish as they may now seem. Take, for example, this passage from David James Duncan's memoir, *My Story as Told by Water*. Duncan is now an environmentalist, writer, and avid fly fisherman.

> I was born . . . without a watershed. On a planet held together by gravity and fed by rain, a planet whose every creature depends on water and whose every slope works full-time, for eternity, to create creeks and rivers, I was born with neither . . .
>
> The dehydrated suburbs of my boyhood felt as alien to me as Mars. . . . I didn't rebel against the situation. Little kids don't rebel. That comes later, along with the hormones. What I did was hand-build my own rivers—breaking all neighborhood records, in the process, for amount of time spent running a garden hose. In the beginning, in Southeast Portland, there was nothing much there at all. Dehydrated Martians seemed to cover the place completely. So I would fasten the family hose to an azalea bush at the uphill end of one of my mother's sloping flower beds, turn the faucet on as hard as Mom would allow, and watch hijacked Bull Run River water spring forth in an arc and start cutting a minuscule, audible river down through the

bed. I'd then camp by this river all day.

As my river ran and ran, the thing my mother understandably hated and I understandably loved began to happen: *creation*. The flower-bed topsoil slowly washed away, and a streambed of tiny colored pebbles gradually appeared: a bed that soon looked just like that of a genuine river, complete with tiny point bars and cutbacks, meanders and eddies, fishy-looking riffles, slow pools. It was a nativity scene, really: the entire physics and fluvial genius of Gravity-Meets-Water-Meets-Earth incarnating in perfect miniature. I built matchbook-sized hazelnut rafts and cigarette-butt-sized elderberry canoes, launched them on my river, let them ride down to the gargantuan driveway puddle that served as my Pacific. I stole a three-inch-tall blue plastic cavalry soldier from my brother's Fort Apache set, cut the stock off his upraised rifle so that only the long, flexible barrel remained, tied a little thread to the end of the barrel to serve as a fly line, and sent the soldier fishing. I'd then lie flat on my belly, cheek to the ground, and stare at this U.S. Cavalry dropout, thigh-deep in his tiny river, rifle-rod high in the air, line working in the current; stare till I became him; stare till, in the sunlit riffle, we actually hooked and landed a tiny sun-glint fish. "Shut off that hose!" my mother would eventually shout out the kitchen window. "You've turned the whole driveway into a mudhole!"

Poor woman, I'd think. *It's not a mudhole. It's a tide flat.*

Duncan titles this section "Adoration of a Hose." When he was a child, the garden hose, the water, and the mess all caught his imagination; as an adult he reads his childhood game as an act of worship. Note how Duncan treats his younger self lightly (it's a bit silly to adore a hose) and yet with utmost respect. He trusts his early play to reveal what he has known to be holy and how he first oriented himself to that holiness.

    🙟 *Describe a game you played as a child, especially one you made up. Write the story of playing the game. When you're finished, reflect in writing on the symbolism of the game and its elements. What does the game reveal about your childhood? What does it reveal about your essential nature?*

Often the images that are most compelling (and that potentially unify our writing) come from our early, impressionable years. Duncan's creation of a mudflat doesn't just foretell his future career; it also introduces a *motif* (a recurring idea or image that is developed over the course of a story) that provides structure and continuity. Childhood memories are rife with motifs that grow in complexity and consciousness with age. We can discover a memoir's structural integrity by lingering on significant images.

    🙟 *Consider an image that impressed you as a child (such as a picture on your bedroom wall, an illustration in a book, or a photograph on the mantelpiece). Describe the image in detail. Describe your childhood self taking the image in. Reflect on the symbolism or import the image held for you.*

The first time Duncan had unhindered access to a real creek, not just a garden hose or city culvert, the sight of a large saltwater fish turned his world upside down. It's worth looking closely at how Duncan tells the story. Note how sensual the description is and how

Duncan lets it take up lots of room:

> I felt physically ordered to crawl out on a cantilevered log, set-
> tle belly-down, and watch the pool gyre directly beneath me,
> the foam-starred surface eddying, eddying, till it became a
> vision of night; water-skipper meteors; sun-glint novas. The
> creek would not stop singing. I spun and spiraled, grew foam-
> dazed and gyre-headed. Pieces of the mental equipment I'd
> been taught to think I needed began falling into the pool and
> dissolving: my preference of light to darkness; sense of right-
> side up and upsidedownness, sense of surfaces and edges,
> sense of where I end and other things or elements begin. The
> pool taught nothing but mystery and depth. An increasingly
> dissolved "I" followed the first verb, gravity, down. Yet depth,
> as the dissolved "I" sees it, is also height.
>
> Then, up from those sunless depths, or yet also down
> from foam-starred heavens, a totem-red, tartan-green impos-
> sibility descended or arose, its body so massive and shining,
> visage so travel-scarred and ancient, that I was swallowed like
> Jonah by the sight. I know no better way to invoke the being's
> presence than to state the naked name:
>
> *Coho*. An old male coho, arcing up not to eat, as trout do,
> but just to submarine along without effort or wings; just to
> move, who knows why, through a space and time it created
> for itself as it glided. And as it eased past my face not a body's
> length away, the coho gazed—with one lidless, primordial
> eye—clean into the suspended heart of me: gazed not like a
> salmon struggling up from an ocean to die, but like a Gaelic or
> Kwakiutl messenger dropped down from a realm of gods. . . .

The creek would not stop singing. My bagpipe heart could not stop answering. When you see a magnificent ocean fish confined in small, fresh water, it is always like a dream. And in our dreams, every object, place, and being is something *inside* us. Despite my smallness, ignorance, inexperience, I felt a sudden huge sense of entitlement. This creek and its music, secret world and its messenger, belonged to me completely. Or I to them.

The coho vanished as serenely as it had come, back into depth. But not before its shining eye changed the way I see out of my own. I'd glimpsed a way into a Vast Inside. A primordial traveler through water and time had said, Come.

This first glimpse of the messenger from the "Vast Inside" sets Duncan on a path that leads him to catch hundreds of fish and be moved by thousands of natural encounters. On the surface not much happens: A boy leans over a log and sees a fish. But something inside of Duncan was changed as a result of seeing that coho, and he honors the moment by describing it in detail. This small event from his youth encapsulates the essence of his life and his book: The natural world is holy, it transforms us, and we have a responsibility to preserve it.

TENSE AND POINT OF VIEW

While childhood memories are often bodily, sensual, and graphic, they are also preverbal; thus they present the writer with a dilemma. Should you write from the point of view of your childhood self, keeping your narrative lens closely identified with your self at age eight? Or should you hang on to your adult voice, which allows reflective space? In fact, writers confront this decision whenever we describe any moment other than the recent past. Writing about childhood is a good place to practice working with tense and narrative distance because the time gap between past and present is so significant.

Try writing memories in present tense—as though they are happening *in this moment*. Instead of writing, "I straddled the two-wheeler," write, "I get on my new bike." The present tense feels awkward at first; it's not a "true" tense (of course you aren't hopping on a bike and writing simultaneously). But writing in the present tense brings memories forward with marked clarity. For this reason, present tense is useful in writing first drafts of memoirs. It captures that freshness. You can always revise it back to the past tense later if it feels more natural.

     Write the story of a childhood first (such as the first time you went fishing, rode a bike, had a nightmare, or moved to a new home). Write in the present tense, as though it is happening now. Be sure to show how this first experience changed you, however subtly.

Many writers feel the present tense gives writing more immediacy than the past tense. "I'm angry!" has more urgency than "I was angry!" However, using the present tense in memoir may feel manipulative because it is not an accurate tense to describe past events. There are exceptions, such as flashbacks of trauma, when the past leaps into the present with frightening accuracy and refuses to be categorically shoved into history. In these instances it is possible to use the present tense effectively. Generally, however, the past tense is sufficiently vibrant. Take Duncan's passage for example: It is so energetic that you don't notice the past tense. Not only does the reader feel the press of that moment above the creek, but he or she is also privy to Duncan's adult insights about what was essentially a nonverbal moment. If we could ask the boy Duncan how his day was, "I saw a huge fish!" might be the most he'd say. And we would not find out about the coho speaking to him, how it changed him and started him on a lifelong mission. We would miss how the fish outside felt like a being inside of him, and he inside of it. The adult narrator is better equipped to give language to the language-less experiences of youth. In the past tense, we can layer reflections seamlessly within events, as Duncan does, or we can call attention to the distance with overt commentary: "I didn't have the words for it then, but I now know that fish was a messenger." Distance between the adult narrator and the child character offers us the flexibility to both show and tell.

    Return to the "first time" you wrote about in the previous exercise. Write about the same memory again from scratch, only this time in the past tense. Include all the sensory information from your first draft as well as any adult reflections or insights you would like to add.

The intent is to articulate memories as accurately and colorfully as possible. To bring memories to life in early drafts, use the present tense or a close past-tense narrative lens (one that fully inhabits the child's point of view). Revise your writing later into the past tense and a more distanced narrator (one that permits the adult's perspective) as you reflect more on those early events.

Primary Faith Experiences

David James Duncan is also a master at distinguishing between the raw sensation of spirit he knew as a child and the religious trappings that his family tried to instill in him. His private encounters with water were powerful enough to remain unswayed by a "proper" faith. In this he was richly blessed. The coho's call remained consistent and persuasive. But many people have had primary, organic experiences of sacredness prior to (and often alongside) the inculcation of a religious tradition. The task of mining our early memories often entails sorting through the spiritual experiences that are truly ours (like Duncan's undeniable encounter with the coho) and those that we learned from culture and family. As spiritual memoirists, our mission is to uncover our soul's journey, and the soul, particularly in childhood, is elusive. The way children drink in religion (with its costumes, rituals, language, and doctrines), is often contrary to adult expectations. As the adult narrator of your story, you must shed your jaded or enthusiastic presumptions about religion in order to recapture that childhood perspective.

This is not to say that a child cannot have a genuine spiritual experience within the context of a tradition. As a twelve-year-old, Elie Wiesel sought out cabbalistic instruction despite his father's lack of support because he yearned to be drawn into "eternity, into that time where question and answer would become one." Or I think of a Lutheran pastor student of mine who, at age ten, dressed up as a monk for Halloween. As a preadolescent, Scott Russell Sanders devoured the Bible because his parents fought over booze and money, and he was certain the Bible held healing secrets. But note how unique Sanders' boyhood relationship with the Bible was:

Zippered shut, bound in fake black leather, no heavier than a meatloaf sandwich, it barely filled my outspread hand. Yet when I tugged at the brass cross that served as the zipper pull, and the book sprang open of its own accord like a set of jaws, I found inside a thousand whispery-thin pages containing everything that God had seen fit to say, from the long-ago days when God still spoke in a clear voice.

Later he writes, "The only virgin I knew about was Mary the mother of Jesus, and I thought the label was part of her name, Virgin Mary, like the Babe in front of Ruth." Every religious tradition has some dimension that captures the imagination of children and touches their essential being.

෴ Recall a dimension of your religious tradition that captured your imagination as a child. Describe it as you experienced it then, withholding your adult opinion. If you wish, follow with a paragraph describing your feelings toward this tradition now.

Traditions also have a dark side that, for the sake of conformity or moral propriety, ignores or overrides children's wealth of direct sacred experience. Up until I saw my first illustrated Bible, God was more a soft feeling than a being. Afterwards, it was difficult to "get that white man off my eyeball," to quote Alice Walker. The tension that arises between what you know to be true and what you are taught is rich material. One of my students wrote a gripping description of her family's expectation that she go forward for an altar call during a Southern Baptist revival. She watched with trepidation as the guest preacher pressed brightly manicured fingers onto the foreheads of her peers, working down the line. In response, each of her friends quaked, spoke in tongues, or rolled around on the floor. When the pastor reached her, nothing happened. She did not "receive the spirit." An internal crisis ensued: Was she not good enough? Did she not believe enough? Or was this religion just a show? Every tradition offers a way to comprehend life's mysteries. If your relationship with a tradition is complex or angry or intimate, if it yields an influence on your soul's story, then your initial memories and the tension they illustrate are rich subject matter.

> ❧ *What stories were formative in your childhood? Consider family stories, faith stories, fairy tales, and books. Choose one with particular power. Describe yourself as a child taking the story in. Then explore how the story supported and/or degraded your innate spiritual life.*

CHILDHOOD TRAUMA

When I teach spiritual memoir, I devote an entire class to writing about childhood. Occasionally a student drops the class afterward, saying, "I don't want to go back there! My childhood was horrible and it's done with. When I signed up I wanted to write about my spiritual life, not my past." For these students, there is a brick wall between childhood and adulthood, between a period of vulnerability and a period of personal agency. They are not yet ready to climb over or break down the wall—emotional work that creates a unified story and a whole self. I understand completely. It's agonizing work even with a relatively happy childhood. I wish these students well.

The brave souls who reenter difficult childhoods by writing about them are doing far more than simply creating a literary work. They are witnessing their spirit's continuity. The self they were then is the same self who writes the story today. It is a transformed self perhaps—a self that has grown in myriad ways, has renounced previous values, or has been born again—but that nonetheless traces its memories to the same origin. "There are all those early memories," Willa Cather writes, "one cannot get another set." If you have endured a traumatic childhood, writing may bring memories back in stark detail. You may remember scenes even therapy doesn't elicit, both positive and negative. The gift comes of writing through the pain. Your memoir is able to hold hurt and healing, childhood and adulthood, and the tremendous resilience of the human spirit all in one place. Making a broken life into a whole story is the most powerful act of healing possible.

No matter what your childhood circumstances, your younger self plays a central and worthy role in your story. The spiritual journey takes its first steps in childhood, long before you have the awareness to name or pursue it. When you honor those memories, you honor holiness in its full complexity.

Being in the Body

THE SPIRIT, WRITES MARY OLIVER, likes to dress up in our bodies; it prefers to "plumb rough matter," to reside inside "the dark hug of time," and to revel in tangibility. There is no spiritual memoir that does not, in one form or another, address bodily existence. The soul's life is shaped by ailments, gender, birth, death, exercise, sex, disabilities, mystical encounters, and by breath. We are solid, after all; we are flesh and bones. Every sacred revelation must be reconciled with the spit and guts of creation. What does it mean to be human? What does it mean to inhabit your body with its unique color, size, shape, and sexual passion? What is your physical inheritance? How do you make sense of your own inevitable mortality?

Scientists now believe that memory resides not so much in the brain but in every cell of the body. That may explain why a friend of mine had her first flashback of sexual abuse while sitting in the dentist's chair, her mouth stuffed with cotton, or why a deep massage releases grief stored in the muscles, and a high fever will transport us back to our childish need for a motherly hand on the forehead. Smell especially triggers the past, probably because it is a sense, as Diane Ackerman writes, that "is immediate and undiluted by language, thought or translation." The alkaline scent of chalk dust brings me immediately to my seventh-grade science classroom, where Mr. Zinn filled blackboards in sliding wood frames with meteorological diagrams. The senses bind past to present instantaneously, without warning.

"The universe is made of stories, not atoms," Muriel Rukeyser writes. Bodies carry our immediate history and our heritage; they too are made of stories. Ask any five-year-old about a scar or lost tooth, and he or she will produce an elaborate saga. Children know their bodies are books. The elderly also know this, narrating their days according to aches and bowel movements. But adults, adrift in heady, abstract worlds, often forget that they inhabit bodies—at least until something goes awry. Working with memory requires attention to the body, both in its current state and in its past. Wisdom resides in our feet, muscles, immune system, and sex drive; we ignore it at our peril.

> ᕦ *In what way do you wear your mother's or father's body or carry a grandparent's ailments? Describe a detail about your body and how it binds you to your forebears. How does this physical connection reveal your emotional or spiritual connection?*

Consider, for example, your hands. What does the condition of your fingernails reveal? Mine are soft; I never get enough calcium in my diet. I cut mine short so I can play piano. The fact that I use clippers on my nails, never buff them, and never paint them exposes both my laziness and my scorn for a certain standard of feminine beauty.

Look carefully at the creases in your palms. Do you see a telling convergence or striking image? Katharine Butler Hathaway did and describes it in the opening of her memoir, *The Little Locksmith*:

I have an island in the palm of my right hand. It is quite large and shaped like an almond. To make this island, the fate line splits in two in the middle, then comes together again up toward the Mount of Jupiter. I don't know what an island means in palmistry. No two people ever interpret it alike. But it looks to me, and that is quite enough for me, as if it meant that a quiet respectable fate were suddenly going to explode in the middle of life into something entirely new and strange, and then be folded together again and go on as quietly as it began. And because something of this kind has happened to me I get a rather foolish magic-loving satisfaction from believing that my island represents that period, the cycle of precious experience which befell me and which I am going to write about in this book. I treasure that little thing in my hand. I pore over it reminiscently, gratefully. I like to know it is there. It is the lucky coin that saved me. It is the wafer of beneficent magic that made everything all right at last. It is the yeast that made my life rise.

Examine your knuckles—are they thick or fine? Pinch the skin on the back of your hand; does it stand upright with age or retract with youthful elasticity? What have your hands accomplished that brings you delight? What have they done that you are ashamed of? When were they strained and broken or patted and pampered? How do you hold them when you pray? Look at your hands as a metaphor—as the means by which your soul reaches into the world. What do and don't they touch? How do they reveal the sacred?

Your hands alone hold enough stories to fill a book, and each chapter would be holy. Internally and externally, our bodies are in constant motion and continual transformation. The cycles of creation manifest themselves in growth, health, and decline. The greatest of mysteries resides in our capacity to produce life. As the Buddha said, "Our body is precious. It is a vehicle for awakening."

What part of your body do you resist writing about? Your bellybutton? Your genitals? Your body hair? Describe that part anyway. Reflect on why you consider it off-limits. In what ways are these feelings connected to or disconnected from your spiritual life?

Why is it then that we frequently shun the body in our living and in our writing? The body reminds us of our imperfections, our brokenness, our mortality, and the irresolvable puzzle of being alive. Essentially we exist in relationship to our bodies, but it is rare in American culture that this relationship is given the positive attention and nourishment required to be healthy. I was twenty-two years old before I realized I could listen to my body. I had spent over twelve hours on my bike riding through mountains in Wales. By the end of the day I had lost control of the muscles in my hands and forearms. I couldn't even spread cream cheese evenly on to crackers. Facing for the first time the likelihood that my body was not inexhaustible, it occurred to me that I had been getting signals all day long—the back ache, the sore rear, the stomach cramp from hunger. Had I listened and attended, I would not have arrived at my miserable state. I promised my body that I would pay closer attention from that moment on.

Choose a part of your body that elicits strong emotion. Writing quickly and without thinking too much, enter into conversation with that part. Allow it to speak on the page. Ask it questions. What might this part of your body have to teach you? What might you teach it?

As writers of spiritual memoir, we have a responsibility to listen to our bodies—for the sake of the story, for our own sake, and for our readers. Whether you like it or not, you are the main character of your story and your body is the means by which the main character walks around in the world. Like any other details that emerge in your story, your emotional and physical responses to events have potential to reveal the story's heart. Because we often ignore the body, it is frequently a storehouse of unrealized insight and, therefore, a rich source of self-discovery in the writing process.

Our bodies ground us to the earth. When we write our bodies, we ground our readers as well. Readers need to know about physical sensation for the story to feel real. Consider the following paragraph about my practice of meditation:

> Every morning I kneel before a candle, close my eyes, and attempt once again to quiet the relentless turbulence of my mind. At first my day's agenda storms across the foreground, thrusting many tasks and responsibilities forward to receive their requisite, stressful attention. "Okay," I reply to the lesson plans, the overgrown lawn, the looming deadline, "I hear you." Then I wait for the turmoil to settle. Occasionally a pocket of quiet emerges, but as soon as I notice it, it's gone. I wish I could float free of this tether to consciousness.

Not a bad paragraph. But now read the revision, which pays closer attention to the body:

Every morning I bend down to my knees in a pool of morning sun. I strike a match, breathe in its burning sulfur, and touch the tip to a candle's wick. The flame gets lost in the day's brilliance. Once again, I attempt to quiet the relentless turbulence of my mind. The wooden prayerstool is hard against my tailbone; I correct my natural slouch into a more upright posture that might sustain me through this half-hour meditation. Then I shut my eyes. At first my day's agenda storms across my mind, thrusting tasks and responsibilities forward to receive their requisite, stressful attention. "Okay," I reply to the lesson plans, the overgrown lawn, the looming deadline, "I hear you." Then I wait for the thoughts to settle. In my lap, my hands shift, seeking a resting place. Occasionally I emerge into a pocket of quiet, but as soon as I notice, it's gone. Mostly I sit, stiff, restless, attending the expansion of my chest with every intake of breath, and the release, the emptying, the silent rush of air. I want to inhale eternity. I want to exhale my self into silence, to throw aside my busy brain with all its burdens and, even for a minute, float free of this tether to consciousness.

The difference between the two paragraphs is subtle, but arguably significant for the reader. The first resides largely in the mind, while the second features the body prominently as the means by which meditation is experienced. On the page, meditation easily becomes an abstract subject. Effort and quiet swirling through the mind's recesses are blurry and abstract. In reality meditation is essentially physical: The back aches, the knees creak, and always there is the tidal flow of breath. When you're writing it's easy to forget that every dimension of your spiritual life is enacted in the body. But the reader, consciously or not, perks up if you include the body. Physical details spark sensation in the reader's body, making the reading experience visceral and sensory. Images cinematically appear in the reader's mind. In fact, sensual details do the same for the writer's body in the midst of writing, making recollections that much more animated. In the middle of writing a scene, ask yourself, What did my body experience in this moment? This will help you stay grounded in the tangible.

> ❧ *Spend a few moments breathing deeply. Describe your breath. What happens to your body? What changes take place as you breathe? Once you've described your breath, free associate. What does your breath remind you of? Where is the sacred in relationship to your breath?*

The following examples from two spiritual memoirs feature the body prominently. The first is from Gretel Ehrlich's memoir, *A Match to the Heart: One Woman's Story of Being Struck by Lightning*. Ehrlich's story of recovery is both physical and spiritual. What does it mean to be struck by lightning, not once but twice? Ehrlich looks closely at her body for clues:

> If I held a match to my heart, would I be able to see its workings, would I know my body the way I know a city, with its internal civilization of chemical messengers, electrical storms, cellular cities in which past, present, and future are contained, would I walk the thousand miles of arterial roadways, branching paths of communication, and coiled tubing for

waste and nutrients, would I know where the passion to live and love comes from?

Ehrlich reads the mechanical workings of her body to learn the origins of her will to survive. In the brief opening chapter, she describes waking after the lightning strike. She had been on a walk on her Wyoming ranch. When lightning hit, she was thrown to the ground. Her circulatory system collapsed, and she was severely burned, cut, and bruised. Note Ehrlich's attention to every nuance of that experience during what was largely an unconscious state.

> Deep in an ocean. I am suspended motionless. The water is gray. That's all there is, and before that? My arms are held out straight, cruciate, my head and legs hang limp. Nothing moves. Brown kelp lies flat in mud and fish are buried in liquid clouds of dust. There are no shadows or sounds. Should there be? I don't know if I am alive, but if not, how do I know I am dead? My body is leaden, heavier than gravity. Gravity is done with me. No more sinking and rising or bobbing in currents. There is a terrible feeling of oppression with no oppressor. I try to lodge my mind against some boundary, some reference point, but the continent of the body dissolves. . . .
>
> A single heartbeat stirs gray water. Blue trickles in, just a tiny stream. Then a long silence.
>
> Another heartbeat. This one is louder, as if amplified. Sound takes a shape: it is a snowplow moving grayness aside like a heavy snowdrift. I can't tell if I'm moving, but more blue water flows in. Seaweed begins to undulate, then a whole kelp forest rises from the ocean floor. A fish swims past and

looks at me. Another heartbeat drives through dead water, and another, until I am surrounded by blue.

Sun shines above all this. There is no pattern to the way its glint comes free and falls in long knives of light. My two beloved dogs appear. They flank me like tiny rockets, their fur pressed against my ribs. A leather harness holds us all together. The dogs climb toward light, pulling me upward at a slant from the sea.

I have been struck by lightning and am alive.

This is an excellent example of describing the indescribable. The metaphor of rising from underwater helps Ehrlich depict the nebulous state between blackout and waking—a time when she was not alert enough to attach language to sensation. Why does Ehrlich bother describing this moment? She doesn't remember the instant of being struck by lightning at all; it takes awhile before she even realizes what has happened. She awakens to a reality forever transformed. It's worth attempting to give it words because it is a birth, a beginning. It's where her story of recovery starts.

Notice how Ehrlich gives her experience to the reader—through her body, through the ocean metaphor, and through her choices in sentence structure. Her appendages are limp; her body is heavier than gravity. When her heart beats, it is such a remarkable sensation it receives its own paragraph. She uses sentence fragments to convey her brokenness and the disjointed quality of time. Her question—how do I know I am dead?— conveys a sense of groping for consciousness. The image of sun coming through the water "in long knives of light" parallels both her pain and the sensation of being beneath awareness.

As best as she is able, she places her readers in her body so that we, too, might know the horror of surviving a lightning strike.

Ehrlich's passage is evidence that the silent, multidimensional life of the body can be conveyed with language—and ought to be if we are to do full justice to our experiences. When direct description fails, metaphorical language can fill the gaps. What was the sensation *like*? For Matthiessen, a moment of enlightenment during meditation is like a great, internal smile. Tom Junod, author of "Can You Say Hero?" knew grace when his "heart felt like a spike, and then . . . opened and felt like an umbrella." For Francis Rothluebber in *Nobody Owns Me*, her "cellobody has deeper notes and wilder music than I ever dreamed. I'm learning to breathe as one with my body the way a cellist does." We can reach outside our bodies for images that unpack the mysteries inside.

Ehrlich's passage also shows how stylistic choices—the length of sentences and paragraphs, the structure and type of sentences, word choice, etc.—help convey the indescribable. A sentence fragment *feels* broken to the reader; a run-on sentence *feels* rushed or excited. Lengthy Latin-based words feel more intellectual and abstract than the earthy, punchy words from Germanic roots (*offensive* versus *stink*; or *imperfect* versus *marred*). As Carol Bly writes, there is a reason people don't shout, "Copulate thee!" The maxim "show, don't tell" applies to language as well as to content.

In his memoir, *Heaven's Coast*, Mark Doty writes about his reverence for the body. "Wally's body was the vehicle through which I knew him," Doty writes of his partner. "All other knowledges proceed through the body, *after* it, as it were. His was a wonderful vehicle, a beloved one, but it was not him. This fact seems so strange to me, so heavily laden, a deep vein of the incomprehensible."

To Doty, bodies are the means by which love is formed and the other is known. And yet our being continues beyond the body. He tracks this "vein of the incomprehensible" as far as he can, as in this passage about Wally immediately after his death:

> There was a deep calm to his face; he seemed a kind of unfathomable, still well which opened on and down beneath the suddenly smooth surface of his skin. Which seemed polished, as it cooled, though not stiff; it was as if his body moved toward the condition of marble, but marble that's been palmed and warmed, touched until it picks up something of human heat. The heat in him lasted a long time. I loved that heat. I don't know how long I held his face and his shoulders and stroked him; as he began to cool I kept my hands on his belly, where the last of his warmth seemed to pool and concentrate. Here the fire of the body came to rest, smoldering longest, down to the last embers.

Rather than turning away from this agonizing instant, Doty allows Wally's body to speak to him. Later Doty writes, "I have never felt so far inside my life, and Wally's." His attention to Wally as the "fire of the body" slowly dwindles brings him to the essence of life, vibrant with loss and connection. Detailing this memory, Doty conveys that essence across time into the reader's life. Wally's body becomes a vehicle for us as well, conveying the enigma of being that survives even death.

Gloria Steinem once said, "If we bless our bodies, they will bless us." Your work as a spiritual memoirist is to bless the body with thoughtful regard, looking for scars and beauty marks, listening for inner grumbling, discerning dimensions of physical sensation, and seeking revelation in pain, pleasure, and growth. If you bless your body in your writing, it will bless your story with its acute senses. As Margaret Atwood says, writing is reverse incarnation—flesh made word. Flesh will always be our beginning point.

Honoring Teachers

WHEN THOMAS MERTON first began dabbling in Catholicism as a young adult, his friend Lax asked him casually, "What do you want to be, anyway?" Merton's first thoughts were a *New York Times* book reviewer or English professor, but then he answered the question more honestly: "I guess what I want is to be a good Catholic."

"What you should say," Lax responded, "is that you want to be a saint."

Merton's reaction was much as you can imagine—this idea was so far-fetched, so removed from what he knew of his weaknesses and limitations, that he dismissed it offhand. But Lax pushed it further: "All that is necessary to be a saint is to want to be one. Don't you believe that God will make you what He created you to be, if you will consent to let Him do it? All you have to do is desire it." Merton finally understood what Lax was getting at and began to sink into his desire.

The first time I read this passage in Merton's memoir, *The Seven Storey Mountain*, I put the book down and sat quietly for a good while. Lax's words reached out through the specifics of Merton's story into my own, challenging me to attend my desires as a place of God's unfolding. It had never before occurred to me that my wanting might be a divine tool for bringing about magnificence. It was a casual comment, but Lax became Merton's teacher in that moment, as well as mine in my moment of reading. I remain grateful for his insight.

> ᏍᎳ *Make a list of people who have contributed to your spiritual development in simple and profound ways. Then, as concisely as possible, write down the primary lesson each person taught you.*

Spiritual teachers show up at odd, passing moments and in long-term positions of importance; we know them through books, casual encounters in the grocery store, and mentorships that last a lifetime. Invariably teachers find their way into our memoirs, where we're able to record their wise words, patience, and the generous way they've pushed us to become more perfectly ourselves. Whenever I read *Seven Storey Mountain* I am reminded of the man who gave the book to me. He was a member of the board of the retreat center where I worked for a number of years—a quiet Scandinavian pastor who paid me the kindness of listening. He taught me that silent receptivity can be more influential in a board meeting than the constant expression of opinion. Life is peopled with teachers. Our spiritual memoir can pay respect to their pervasive influence.

Because teachers play a prominent role in many seekers' journeys, it's no surprise that a great number of spiritual memoirs revolve around teachers and their lessons. This is especially true in traditions that include devotion to a guru (as in Irina Tweedie's *Chasm of Fire*, in which she describes turning her self and will over to her Sufi master), or in which the student/teacher relationship is a primary means for revelation (for example, Natalie Goldberg's emulation of Zen master

Katagiri Roshi in *Long Quiet Highway* and Henri Nouwen's conversations with the Trappist abbot John Eudes in *The Genesee Diary*). Sometimes teachers are divine; sometimes they manifest the divine. Most often they teach us to recognize the divine within ourselves.

In memoir, teachers are characters in a story. It's important to develop them so that they come alive as whole, multifaceted humans. What are your teacher's physical characteristics, speech patterns, and body language? When your teacher says something profound, the significance rests only partly in the words. The remainder depends on nonverbal cues, on your relationship, on the context of the teaching, and on your receptivity. What are the emotional dynamics between you? What do you admire in this person? What don't you understand? Where does the teacher reveal the dark side of humanity? Parents tell children, "Do as I say, not as I do." It's an unrealistic expectation, since actions are far more powerful teachers than words. What does your teacher do?

In *Bones of the Master*, George Crane describes first meeting Tsung Tsai, who became his spiritual guide. A freak snowstorm had littered the woods with broken branches and both men were out clearing the road:

> I walked across the yard to meet him, wet snow crunching under my boots. "I am Tsung Tsai," he introduced himself. "Neighbor. Old monk. Buddhist," he added.
>
> "George Crane." I stuck out my hand.
>
> "Ahh, Georgie name." He nodded and grabbed my hand with his—warm, hard-callused, and thick-fingered. "You are writer."
>
> "How did you know?"

He set his ax into a tree stump and settled the saw next to it. "I don't know. Just guess."

Even in this simple scene, note how the setting, Tsung Tsai's accent and actions, and the physical details all work to introduce Tsung Tsai as a flesh-and-bones person who also has extraordinary intuition. When Crane creates his first portrait of Tsung Tsai, it is strikingly frank:

> He was a few inches shorter than I, and about twenty years older: a small man, five foot five, solid, maybe 140 pounds. His large ears curled away from his head and stuck out from under a yellow watch cap. He was dressed in an eccentric collection of rags: a buttonless brown cardigan sweater and a zipperless thrift store parka that leaked polyester fill. Underneath he wore a cinnamon-colored cotton jacket; the pockets I could see were closed with safety pins. His thin cotton pants were the color of tea and tied at the ankles with shoelaces. Against the wet snow, he wore a child's pair of yellow rubber boots.

It's especially important when crafting a portrait of a spiritual teacher to pay tribute with honesty. Attempts to honor the teacher with only glowing admiration backfire, making readers distrustful of the narrator and skeptical about the superstar guru. Crane's straightforward, almost comical depiction of his teacher conveys both realism and reverence. Although it might not seem so at first, it is far more respectful to describe your teacher's warts alongside his wisdom, her mistakes alongside her miraculous capabilities. Your teacher inhabits a body like the rest of us, has a history, and will someday die. Attending to these details in your story brings the character of your teacher back down to earth, where readers can relate to him or her.

> ❧ *Write a portrait of your teacher or a significant person in your spiritual journey. Remember to include body language, quality of voice, clothing, tics, etc. If appropriate, describe the teacher's physical surroundings as well. Can you capture the essence of this person by showing him or her in relationship or in action?*

A strange phenomenon occurs in portraiture: We intend to reveal or celebrate a subject and instead wind up disclosing far more about ourselves. A grand example of this is found in Tom Junod's endearing short memoir, "Can You Say Hero?" Junod sets out to profile Fred Rogers, shadowing him for a few weeks as he shoots episodes of *Mister Rogers' Neighborhood*. From the start Junod asks, "What makes Mr. Rogers so good? What keeps him going?" Junod swims laps with Rogers, and describes him in the locker room as "gnawed pink in the spots where his dry skin has gone to flaking, slightly wattled at the neck, slightly stooped at the shoulder, slightly sunken in the chest, slightly curvy at the hips . . . and yet when he speaks, it is in *that* voice, *his* voice, the famous one, the unmistakable one, the televised one, the voice dressed in sweater and sneakers. . . ." Junod shows Rogers growing tired, defying his staff, stooping down to listen to children, signing photographs with the Greek word for grace, and peeing at the edge of a cemetery. It's a complex portrait; it jolts us by peeling away Mr.-Rogers-the-icon to expose the man. As a result, Mr. Rogers is not a flat caricature but a real person with whom the reader can relate.

In one scene, Rogers asks Junod to tell him about the stuffed rabbit he lost as a boy at the same time he lost his faith in prayer.

And it was just about then, when I was spilling the beans about my special friend, that Mister Rogers rose from his corner of the couch and stood suddenly in front of me with a small black camera in hand. "Can I take your picture, Tom?" he asked. "I'd like to take your picture. I like to take pictures of all my new friends, so that I can show them to Joanne. . . ." And then, in the dark room, there was a wallop of white light, and Mister Rogers disappeared behind it.

Try as he might, Junod cannot keep the spotlight pointed at Fred Rogers because Rogers keeps pointing it back at him. This is always the case with portraiture. Portraits reveal more about the writer than about the subject because through the description of the subject, the author's sensibilities are exposed. We see through the author's eyes, we note what he notes, we wonder what he wonders. Perhaps this is more obvious with visual art; certainly we learn more about Degas from his paintings than we do about the dancers. When you portray a teacher in memoir, the lens you use always reveals yourself to the reader.

> ୶ *Return to the portrait you created for the previous exercise. Ask yourself, "How do my choices—what I noticed, how I described it—reveal my own personality and values?" Be aware of the subtext that resides in the portrait. Later, when you revise the descriptions of characters, intentionally reveal the parts of yourself that point toward your story's heartbeat.*

Teachers, more so than other characters in our memoirs, have a tendency to dominate our stories. Writers often give them reams of dialogue. We examine their words with great care. We love to describe the teachers' attributes because we love *them*, and the memoir is a chance to lavish them with praise. But once you write down your adoration, consider its role in the larger story. Adoration is never the solitary purpose of memoir. Rather, the purpose is to uncover the sacred, honor it, and share it with others. To uncover the sacred within someone you admire, you must carefully examine that admiration. What qualities does your teacher possess that you respect? How do you understand these same qualities within yourself? How, exactly, does your teacher make the sacred more available to you? By articulating the emotional and spiritual dimensions of your relationship, you open the possibility of further discovery and make your experience more available to the reader.

A student of mine was working on her memoir about studying Buddhism; she was particularly interested in relaying the teachings of her Zen master. In an early draft, the master gives a dharma talk, which runs for many pages. Reading it, I became distracted and was unable to follow the teacher's logic. I asked the writer to revise the scene; I suggested she interrupt the dialogue with physical descriptions of the teacher, the setting, and her own body. When I read the second draft, I was pleased to learn that the writer was just as restless listening to her teacher as I was—her legs cramped, her thoughts wandered. It wasn't until years later that she grasped the meaning of the dharma talk. Knowing this, I was more patient with my own thick-headedness; I felt the press of the zaffu cushion, the zendo's close air, and the hush of the master's voice. I sensed the master's confident but quiet presence. The dharma talk became a physical experience for me and—pleasant surprise!—I was able to grasp its import. At first, everything but the teacher's wise words seemed irrelevant to the writer, but on further reflection the words in their pure form were inaccessible, even to her.

The complete experience of the teacher's lesson, including how the writer digested the lesson, is necessary to pass the experience along to the reader.

      From the list you made of significant people and their lessons, choose one person/lesson that has energy for you. Write a scene showing you in relationship to this person, learning the lesson. Describe the teacher, the student, the setting, and the circumstances. As concretely as possible, show the learning process.

Beginning writers of spiritual memoir often turn over their narrative authority to their teachers by relying heavily on quotations. You know the impulse—someone else has said what you mean with such panache and brevity that you couldn't possibly use your own clumsy words. So you insert a quotation, thus relinquishing your authority, your voice, your experience. If you are overtaken by this impulse in a first draft, go for it. But as you revise be sure to examine your use of quotations. When a quotation is central to your experience, when it spurs your journey and you've taken time to reflect on the intersection between its sagacity and your transformation, chances are good that the quotation works well in the story. But if a quotation is an escape from the hard work of articulating your own insights, most likely it detracts from the story and ought to be cut. Your words, as unadorned as they may seem, carry greater meaning and intimacy.

      Practice claiming your authority by taking a quotation that has been important to you and rewriting it in your own words. Then write about an experience that led you to arrive at this piece of wisdom. Can your story show what the original quote tells?

As wise as your teacher may be, he or she is not the locus of wisdom in your memoir. You are. Your story is the container; your voice is the guide; your personality is the principal way your reader will inhabit your world. As far as the reader is concerned, your teacher is only relevant inasmuch as he or she informs your life. This is equally true whether your teacher is Mohammed himself or the homeless woman on the street. If your teacher discloses the secret to eternal bliss, it makes no difference to the story unless that secret has an impact on your life. Take Robert Johnson's moment of despair in Calcutta from *Balancing Heaven and Earth*:

> Each street . . . seemed to be worse than the last, until I became inundated with the darkness and the agony of India . . . . In the next block, a woman dressed in filthy, tattered clothes pushed a dead baby into my arms while begging for money. Next I encountered small children poking me with amputated arms and withered legs. I could not find a building that looked safe, and I began to lose my composure. I was one thousand miles from anyone I knew and felt myself falling into an abyss. It was worse than a panic attack; it was as if I had wandered into some corner of hell.
>
> . . . Then I remembered that there was something to do. I had once been told by a friend that in India you have the right to approach a stranger and ask that person to be the incarnation of God. . . . This person may refuse the request, but generally it is considered a sacred duty to accept the role if he or she possibly can because it is an honor and such a profound experience. . . . Only worship and reverence are

appropriate in such a relationship; you must not ask for anything else from the person but that he or she serves as the incarnation of god for you.

Luckily, I had tucked away my knowledge of this custom somewhere in the back of my brain. I could see trees off in the distance, and I walked several more blocks until I reached a tiny park. Then I began desperately looking for someone I could approach and ask to be my incarnation of God. I spotted a middle-aged man; he was dressed in Indian fashion and was barefoot, but he had an air of dignity and calmness. I am amazed now at my boldness, but I was driven by desperation. I approached him.

"Sir, do you speak English?"

"Yes."

"Would you be the incarnation of God for me?"

"Yes," he replied, without losing his dignity at my extraordinary request.

It is a staggering thought that he would understand and accept this; all I had to do was ask the question. He pointed me to a bench, and for the next twenty minutes I poured out my woes, telling him who I was and how Calcutta had worn me down, that I felt as if I would soon disintegrate. He said not a word but listened patiently to me. I continued to lay out this burden that was too much for me to experience by myself, and gradually I began to feel calmer. It was as if the burden was halved in sharing it with him, and half of it I could cope with. He really didn't have to say a word, just listen to me, and that is what he did. Eventually I regained my wits; I wasn't happy, but I could function again. As soon as I could, I thanked him, at which point he stood up and bowed.

The anonymous man in the park becomes a temporary container for Johnson's story. Essentially this is the literary role the teacher-character plays in every spiritual memoir. The teacher is a vessel that, for a period of time, shapes and holds the author's story. Only the *contents* of the vessel—your personhood, your life—will quench your reader's thirst.

Journeys

ONE DAY I left the house with a pair of scissors. After a seemingly eternal winter, the crabapple trees were canopies of pink, the grass blindingly green, and the soil alive with earthworms. In my front yard I cut narcissus, glad for their sunny faces. And in the backyard, along the alley, I entered the lilac's sweet realm; I reached between the branches to snip three generous sprigs. Their scent buzzed in my head and made the afternoon reel. Coming into the house, I heard the screen door slam behind me. For an instant the kitchen was dark and formless, but then my eyes adjusted. The lilacs in my hand sugared the air, the narcissus brought in sunshine, and for the first time this season my home was consecrated with color.

It doesn't take much to go on a journey. You leave a place of familiarity, encounter the world, and return changed. The most ancient metaphor for life is a journey, and there's no dimension of experience that cannot be understood within the journey framework. Certainly each minuscule spiritual venture (each foray into doubt, each intentional walk around the block, each worship service or sesshin) is a journey, inasmuch as we are transformed, however slightly. It takes very little for the heart to travel outside of its comfort zone and be moved. Whenever we leave home to encounter newness, we embark on a journey.

> ✒ *Write about a moment of departure, small or large. Be sure to include the sensations of the moment. What was known? What was unknown? What did you fear? Expect? What did you carry with you? Where were you going? In hindsight, where did you actually go?*

When does a journey become spiritual? There are occasions when we set out with the intention of nourishing the soul, when we seek insight (in the landscape, in a holy site, in a guru) and follow our longings beyond the borders of the familiar. George Crane does this in *Bones of the Master*, traveling with his teacher to China to pay homage to a lost monastic tradition. In *The Snow Leopard*, Matthiessen travels to the Himalayas with a field biologist, ostensibly to find the snow leopard but also seeking peace with what is. During my last year of college, I saw myself falling into a pattern of stagnation and self-effacement; I took a semester in Wales to bike the mountains with the hope that I would learn how to listen to my spirit. These journeys are conscious and deliberate; they are the equivalent of a retreat or midday walking meditation. On spiritual journeys, we expect transformation, we open ourselves to movement.

But then there are occasions when we're blundering along without any intention of spiritual growth and new awareness bursts through regardless. You're in a poor country for the first time, and suddenly see your own luxuries as meaningless. Or you are struck with an illness that forces you to question your life's purpose. Although a certain amount of open-heartedness is necessary for newness to break upon us, the sacred can catch us by surprise. My favorite example is Dennis Covington's story *Salvation on Sand Mountain.* Covington was a reporter assigned to cover the trial of an Appalachian snake-handling pastor who was accused (and found guilty) of attempting to murder his wife with poisonous snakes. Covington followed the travels and worship of this pastor's congregation, The Church of Jesus with Signs Following. The members played tambourines, drank strychnine, handled snakes, spoke in tongues, and drove to remote towns and mountaintops to preach the Word. A disenfranchised, mainline Methodist, Covington could not deny these folks' deep-rooted faith, even in light of their leader's corruption, and gradually found himself experiencing a spiritual renewal. During one outdoor revival, he actually felt the arm-waving ecstasy he'd previously only observed. What began as a reporting job gradually became a spiritual journey.

    ✑ *Recall a small journey you've taken. As you write the story of this journey, be aware of how the external journey mirrored your soul's journey.*

A simple definition of a spiritual journey is when both your physical self and your soul move. External changes have their counterparts in our thoughts, feelings, and beliefs. When I was biking through Snowdonia in Wales, my sense of living a metaphor was eerie. I'd head up a mountain, legs straining, gut cramped, pushing my physical capacity; meanwhile, inside, I scaled a mountain of loneliness as I learned to trust my abilities and my emotional limitations. On the ride downhill, I knew both physical freedom and the power of self-determination. When I crossed the border into England, I felt distanced from myself, and when I crossed back into the harsh mountains of my ancestors' country, I knew I was home. The road became an external manifestation of my inner transformation.

Intense journeys like my biking trip or any fresh encounter with a new culture or landscape have great potential for spiritual memoir. For one thing, we're physically in motion, and this requires awareness of our bodies. When we travel, we are removed from the familiar and become absorbed outside of ourselves—in the smells, language, plants, and people around us. We're all eyes, ears, and surprised palates. This absorption has a childlike quality; our memories of travel often have the same vibrancy as memories of childhood. The self-lessness of travel can make us vulnerable and open in ways we may not comprehend until we've taken time to give the memories form.

   Think of a moment when you were moving (walking, biking, flying, driving) as part of a journey. Describe the sensation of movement, of leaving one place on your way to another. Connect the physical sensation with a movement you experienced in your spirit.

The link between the tangible world we discover on a journey and the intangible, responsive changes that occur within makes for energetic writing. Physical journeys provide a natural form—a beginning (leaving), middle (moving), and end (returning)—that is mythic in quality and reminiscent of many holy stories, from Siddhartha's venture outside the palace walls to the Jews' crossing the wilderness to the Mormons' migration westward. Journeys provide a rolling narrative; we can't help but wonder what happens next. Because our readers know we've traversed a literal landscape, they intuit that we've traversed a landscape of psyche or soul as well, and they are eager to know what it looks like. It's often the case that the writer hasn't a clue what the inner landscape looks like until the details of the journey surface on the page.

   ❧ Describe an object or souvenir that you picked up on a journey—particularly if it's something you stumbled upon rather than sought out. Tell the story of where and how you came upon this object. What does it now symbolize to you about your journey?

We can uncover the spiritual nature of a journey by asking the question, What changed? Bringing lilacs and narcissus into my home changed the atmosphere and altered my awareness of spring. Change isn't always positive, however. Some journeys lead us astray before turning toward our real destination. Even so, if we closely examine the transformation that occurred, comparing the "before" portrait of ourselves with the "after," describing the intricate factors that have brought us from here to there, we touch on something essential and true.

The question, What changed? requires that you begin your story with a clear picture of who you were at the start of the journey. Without a good look at the beginning place, you have nothing against which to measure growth. When I set out on my cycling trip, my calves were flabby and I'd never biked more than thirty miles in a day—and that over flat Minnesota prairie. It's important for the reader to know this in order to appreciate how strong I was by the end. Likewise, the ✔ reader needs to know my initial lack of self-certainty and insecure standing with God in order to recognize the significance of my eventual boldness and rooted faith. A self-portrait at the beginning of a story usually requires flashbacks to fill the reader in on what led you to venture out in the first place. Memoir requires a patient, gentle rendering of the person you were when the journey was launched. It's just like the "before" and "after" photographs in diet ads; you need the comparison to appreciate the diet's success. The significance of any journey is measured against its starting place.

    ❮❯ *Write three brief self-portraits, as though they are snapshots: one of you at the start of a journey, one in the midst of journeying, and one at the end.*

Searching for the agent of change drives you into the story's heart. Here is where the real mystery resides for the writer: You may know what happened to you, but you don't see how or why. Any slight factor that instigated transformation is worth describing. Was it the sunshine that moved me on the day I cut the flowers? Was it the brilliant color and scent entering my house after a stale winter? Was it the juice of life blooming in the lilacs that reminded me of my own blessed vitality? Lest you think probing the details of your journey is boring for the reader, and lest you assume the reader wants to leap ahead to the end, consider this: By recreating the experience of being changed, of changing, you give the reader access to that transformation. People don't read spiritual memoirs to find out how wise the writers became in the end; we read to learn how the the writers gained that wisdom. Your story can give readers more tools for making the journey themselves. Take your time writing the middle part of your journey; it is the story's meat.

Andre Dubus's short memoir, "Love in the Morning," illustrates this point. Dubus describes his habit of going to morning mass and then doing laps outside the church in his wheelchair. He repeatedly passes workers on break at a nursing home and people gathering for an Alcoholics Anonymous meeting. He describes singing aloud, sweating, stopping to drink water. When a strange man approaches, Dubus describes the event in detail:

> His overcoat was unbuttoned, and he wore a coat and white shirt and tie; he had lost hair above his brow, and something about his face made me feel that he did not work in an office. I turned to roll in front of the church; he was walking parallel to me, thirty feet away, and he looked at me. I stopped singing. He was glaring, and I felt a soft rush of fear under my heart, and a readying of myself. He raised his right arm and his middle finger and yelled: "Fuck God."
>
> He was looking at the church, walking fast, his finger up. My fear changed; for a moment I expected a response: the sky suddenly dark gray, thunder, lightning. He yelled it again. We were both opposite the church door, and there was no fear in me now; I wondered if any of the alcoholics or if the priest in the rectory were frightened or offended. He yelled again, his finger up; his anger was pure and fascinating. . . . As I pushed to the top of the parking lot, I looked up at the nursing home. The workers had gone inside. I sang, and laughed as I rolled past the rear of the church, seeing all of us: the roofs of the church and rectory, and the alcoholics talking and smoking, and me singing and sweating in the wheelchair, and the man in the suit and tie, with his finger up as far as he could reach. On that morning under a blue November sky, it was beautiful to see and hear such belief: Fuck *God.*

Dubus takes his time describing these mundane observations from his workout because he knows his insights into belief were born of his repetitive laps, the congregating strangers, and the angry man. His encounters with these people and daily participation in the Eucharist form the content of his journey. It is necessary for Dubus to relate all of these observations for the reader to arrive with him at the end:

> I go to mass because the Eucharist is there. . . . It fills the church. If the church had no walls, the Eucharist would fill the parking lot, the rectory, the nursing home, the football stadium. And the church has no walls, and the Eucharist fills the women smoking outside the nursing home; and the alcoholics waiting to gather, but they are gathered, as they are gathered when they are apart; fills the man cursing God from the isolation of his mind. . . . When I am enclosed by the walls and roof and floor, and the prayers and duration of mass, I see this, and feel it; and when the priest places the host in the palm of my hand, I put it in my mouth and taste and chew and swallow the intimacy of God.

Without first hearing about Dubus's laps around the church, we cannot fully understand how this ritual alters him.

Thus we must address the question of what changed at the conclusion of our story, in the context of reintegrating ourselves into home and community. What difference does it make that you took a journey? How does the journey still shape and inform you? What physical evidence of it remains—photos, souvenirs, journals, a polished stone—that continues to travel with you? Ground your readers in the consequences of your journey to help them arrive.

Initially, when I reflected on my tiny journey into the backyard, I didn't give the five minutes of cutting flowers much thought. As I relived and penned the journey, however, I grew aware for the first time of how the narcissus and lilacs changed the air in my house. While I enjoyed cutting and arranging them in vases, it wasn't until I wrote the story that I realized it was a soulful moment. The journey was spiritual, but I was unaware of this quality until I wrote it out.

Writing invites heightened attention. Often holiness lies hidden until we tend it with listening and language. As Wendell Berry says, "The world cannot be discovered by a journey of miles, no matter how long, but only by a spiritual journey, a journey of one inch, very arduous and humbling and joyful, by which we arrive at the ground at our feet and learn to be at home." The miles we've traveled and described are a means for discovering that single, blessed inch.

The Significance of Setting

WHEN I WAS YOUNG I spent hours sitting in the living-room rocker staring out the window over the Hudson River. First there was our dappled lawn, hemmed by tulip trees and hemlocks. Beyond that, a length of swamp tossing its feathered tassels in great, swirling sweeps made way for the railroad bed, a uniform mound of gravel topped with shimmering rails. And finally there was the river, two miles wide, cut through by barges and kicking up whitecaps—always shifting and dangerous. I watched military ships plow their route north to West Point, their decks neat and flags trim. I followed the trail of cloud shadows as they streaked across the gray surface of the river. In those thoughtless, absorbed moments, the river imprinted itself on me. Its continuous splash and hush was my lullaby; its far reach became my thinking space. Fortunately my parents had as much appreciation for the view as I did and permitted my idleness. Who I am is indelibly marked by that river. The Hudson defined home for me. Today, when it appears in my dreams, I feel visited by God.

     Draw a map of a landscape from your childhood (maybe your neighborhood, your grandparents' farm, or a city park where you played often). Then label the places where stories happened. What stories surprise or interest you? Write these, paying particular attention to their settings.

Place, novelists are fond of saying, is as much a character as any person inhabiting the story. Indeed, we were all raised by our places of origin. We have inherited those places' aesthetics (mountains are inspirational to Coloradan and claustrophobic to a North Dakotan), language quirks (even after sixteen years in the Midwest, I refuse to call soda "pop"), pace (my Minnesota friends say my New York stride is stressful), cultural values, tolerance for weather, and dozens of other characteristics. More elementally, our places of origin mold our souls in subtle but indelible ways. In *A Walker in the City*, Alfred Kazin roams the Brownsville neighborhood of East Brooklyn where he grew up, returning to the leathery air of the synagogues and the sweating paving stones to discover what first formed his personhood and awakened his senses. Terry Tempest Williams examines the destruction of wildlife along Great Salt Lake as a way to understand the cancer plaguing the women in her family. Her memoir, *Refuge*, reveals how the land roots her to the past and how its pollution may be connected to her family's illness. Surroundings spin themselves into the substance of our being. When we describe place, we unearth the stuff of which we are made.

Describe your landscape of origin — its contours, flora and fauna, architecture, weather, waterways, etc. In what ways do you understand the landscape that shaped you? In what ways have you rebelled against it?

Kathleen Norris's term *spiritual geography* is useful when we consider the role of place in memoir. In her introduction to *Dakota*, she writes,

> Nearly twenty years ago I returned to the holy ground of my childhood summers; I moved from New York City to the house my mother had grown up in, in an isolated town on the border between North and South Dakota. More than any other place I lived as a child or young adult—Virginia, Illinois, Hawaii, Vermont, New York—this is my spiritual geography, the place where I've wrestled my story out of the circumstances of landscape and inheritance. The word "geography" derives from the Greek words for earth and writing, and writing about Dakota has been my means of understanding that inheritance and reclaiming what is holy in it.

All of us "wrestle" our stories "out of the circumstances of landscape," be that landscape a tenement, skyscraper, or sun-bleached plain. My heart's landscape is the Hudson River Valley, but in the meantime I'm in Minnesota, where the open fields and myriad lakes slowly teach me an appreciation of still, horizontal beauty. So I wrestle my story out here in a little stucco bungalow with the city surrounding me, the Mississippi slinking past, and suburbs then farmland expanding in all directions. The places we inherit are like stretches of canvas on which we paint our lives. We are limited by its bounds. We are gifted with its texture and tautness.

   ❧ *Describe the view outside your favorite window. What in this view moves you? Why?*

The term *spiritual geography* implies more than a passive backdrop. The flatlands of Dakota instigate Norris's journey, prodding her to notice weather, bird migrations, and farming cycles. The flatlands open her eyes to the minute and challenge her to find God in the obvious. "Suddenly," Norris writes, "fir trees seem like tired old women stooped under winter coats. I want to be light, to cast off impediments, and push like a tulip through a muddy smear of snow. I want to take the rain to heart, let it move like possibility, the idea of change." The land is her teacher. It becomes a map she reads to traverse her internal landscape.

The spiritual geography of a memoir is the setting. Your relationship to place may be passing or potent, but it nonetheless exists as a dynamic element and must be developed as such. When you're writing, think of place as a character in need of fleshing out on the page in all its stink and clamor and color. The reader needs to know it as viscerally as you do. It's easy to take a setting for granted, forgetting that the reader cannot see your childhood house or the long-sought pilgrimage site. Remembering the angle of sunlight, the temperature of the air, the feel of soil or pavement beneath your feet, and other small details gives a place agency on the page—an agency similar to its original influence. Place becomes a factor to reckon with.

   ꙳ *Choose a place that carries emotional potency for you and dialogue with it. What do you have to say to this place? What does the place have to say to you?*

One great way to overcome writer's block is to describe a landscape. Maybe it's the view out the window above your desk, even if it's not exceptional—a bit of lawn, the street, your neighbors' junker cars and overgrown scrub trees. Or describe a place from whatever memory is relevant to your writing. Although you may have no clue where your story is going and don't know what relevance the setting has, by simply attending to place, some attribute of your story's heart reveals itself. Once I wrote about the scary high school dropout who lives in the house across from me. He harasses me and therefore challenges me to practice loving my neighbor. I described his flabby thighs and sour voice, but I hit a wall. He pissed me off, his antisocial behavior frightened me, and I didn't know what to make of it on the page. I took a break and described the shabby, leaning house he and his mother live in. In sharp contrast to the other tidy bungalows on the block, it's like a child's drawing—flat, with two windows for eyes and the door a shocked mouth. I imagined this house in its poverty had swallowed my bully whole and for the first time felt compassion toward him. By reading the landscape, I gained insight into my subject.

So place, in its tangibility, discloses the intangible. It also serves the important purpose of rooting both you and the reader in the earth. By describing the broken siding of my neighbor's house, I grounded myself in the physical reality of his life and saw that his behavior, while inexcusable, had its origin in poverty. I was able to give my reader the wider picture, within which our drama plays out.

THE NATURAL WORLD

The natural world is where we are most apt to encounter the mystery of creation in its beauty, abundance, and terror. Our spiritual lives are enacted against the backdrop of place, but place, especially the natural world, is not passive. Nature prods us to grow, inspires us with generosity, and uproots us with earthquakes, tornadoes, and devastating floods. The seasons assert their cycle on our psyche; our animal instincts surprise and guide us; the weather affects our moods. No advance in technology will ever remove us from our creaturely origin. Our encounters with the natural world, for good or ill, confront us with ultimate mystery.

The sunset's melting palate and the delicacy of a snowflake are wondrous, but they've been so written to death that it's difficult to do them justice without sounding cliché. A dilemma that often confronts writers is the apparent greeting card quality of our sentiments. But never doubt the potency of your experience. If a sunset truly moved you, then it is possible (although challenging) to describe it in such a way that moves the reader as well. Dig below the standard, obvious response to beauty and uncover your unique, irrefutable reaction. There is no universal experience of the day's close; you cannot assume the reader shares your experience. Do you see the sun sinking below the hills, or do you feel the earth turning away from the sun? Does the expanse of sky make you feel small or enlarged? What memories resonate in this moment? (I, for instance, cannot see orange in a sunset without a moment of panic, recalling the orange fire that once destroyed my belongings.) How does your body respond? What is sacred for you in this moment? The best way to avoid cliché is to find the nuances of your particular experience.

   Consider the natural world surrounding your home. Choose a small piece—a corner of garden, the birdfeeder, a weed in the sidewalk. Describe it in detail. What does this small piece of creation have to tell you about the nature of the sacred?

Annie Dillard is a master of writing about spirituality and the natural world. She is uncompromising in her determination to look closely at nature and describe *what is*, in all its complexity. "We must somehow take a wider view," she writes in *Pilgrim at Tinker Creek*, "look at the whole landscape, really see it, and describe what's going on here. Then we can at least wail the right question into the swaddling band of darkness, or, if it comes to that, choir the proper praise." Here's an example of Dillard doing just that:

> At the end of the island I noticed a small green frog. He was exactly half in and half out of the water, looking like a schematic diagram of an amphibian, and he didn't jump.
>
> He didn't jump; I crept closer. At last I knelt on the island's winterkilled grass, lost, dumbstruck, staring at the frog in the creek just four feet away. He was a very small frog with wide, dull eyes. And just as I looked at him, he slowly crumpled and began to sag. The spirit vanished from his eyes as if snuffed. His skin emptied and drooped; his very skull seemed to collapse and settle like a kicked tent. He was shrinking before my eyes like a deflating football. I watched that taut, glistening skin on his shoulders ruck, and rumple, and fall. Soon, part of his skin, formless as a pricked balloon, lay in floating folds like bright scum on top of the water: it was a monstrous and terrifying thing. I gaped bewildered, appalled. An oval shadow hung in the water behind the drained frog; then the shadow glided away. The frog skin bag started to sink.

Dillard goes on to explain what she has seen—the work of a giant water bug that seizes its victims with hooked forelegs, paralyzes them with poison that dissolves their innards, and sucks them out like juice.

This would simply be attentive nature writing if Dillard did not continue by quoting the Koran (Allah asks, "The heaven and the earth and all in between, thinkest thou I made them in *jest*?") and then responding, "If the giant water bug was not made in jest, was it then made in earnest?" Dillard's relentlessly accurate depiction of "what's going on here" is not told in isolation but rather bound to her spiritual quest and her capacity for reverence. She finds the sacred by eschewing simplistic, idealized notions of the natural world in favor of its harsh, ludicrous glamour.

    🙠 *Brainstorm a list of things found in nature or attributes of the natural world that confound you. (Platypuses? Migration patterns? The fact that some animals eat their young?) Choose one item from the list to which you can attach a specific memory. Write the memory, being sure to include the questions it raises.*

This is good policy for the spiritual memoirist. Our inclination when writing about the natural world is to generalize, simplify, and shun its darkness in favor of its light. Wouldn't you rather write about the rhubarb's growth spurt and the resident vitality in spring bulbs than the blight taking the tomatoes or the decay gnawing at the iris? The point is not to seek out the gruesome or give it undue attention; it is to depict the natural world as both glorious and threatening. To relate one facet at the expense of another does creation a disservice. It's not unlike depicting loved ones: The most respectful portrait is not rosy-lensed but complicated and paradoxical. Our work, then, is to face *what is*, as much as we can. The sacred always resides in fullness. We shun fullness to our own detriment and to the detriment of our stories.

SACRED SPACES

Holy sites can be effective landmarks in a narrative, either along the way or at a journey's climax. Places of worship, burial sites, favorite sitting rocks, pilgrimage destinations, and natural wonders all serve as focal points for awe. We develop a relationship with places, fantasize about them, cherish them, turn to their memories for sustenance, and return to them over time. Long before I first visited Stonehenge, a place with strong gravitational pull on my soul, I engaged it with my imagination, and in the years since my visit, I've honored its image in my memory. I feel great affection and receding bitterness for the small, Protestant-plain church where I grew up. When I worship there every other year or so, the smell of horse-hair carpeting and old paint returns me to my earliest, unadulterated encounters with Christianity. Our relationship to holy places changes as we change, but continues nonetheless.

If you are strongly affected by place, place can become a structural support for your memoir. Michael Dorris traces his relationship to home by telling about the yards from three periods of his life. Terry Tempest Williams uses the rising and receding of the Great Salt Lake to frame her story in *Refuge*. Descriptions of place are touchstones; they guide the reader through the more abstract elements of a story.

> ○∞ *Create a chronological list of the holy sites in your spiritual journey—places of worship, transformation, and pilgrimage. Spend some time describing each place. These sites can povide a structure for your memoir.*

Be wary of assuming that holiness is inherent to a place. A site may very well radiate healing and significance for you and for the millions of pilgrims who have traveled there. But you cannot assume that the place's impact on your spiritual journey is as straightforward as your memory makes it seem. Nor can you assume that the mere mention of this place will convey its potency to your reader. The experience of holiness is bound up in infinite details. To pay as much homage to a holy site in writing as you have paid in your life, you must attend to the details.

For instance, many people have visited Stonehenge and many more consider it a center of ancient power. I spent my childhood devouring any history and mythology I could find about that ancient circle of stones—their origins, theories about the engineering that raised them, the astronomical principles of their layout, and legends of the druids, King Arthur, and Merlin, who treated Stonehenge as a meeting place between this world and the next. On my bedroom wall was a poster of Stonehenge at the full moon, superimposed with Robert Frost's words, "We dance round in a ring and suppose/But the secret sits in the center and knows." Unlike the Methodist church my family attended weekly, which by then had grown too familiar and mundane in my eyes, Stonehenge was mighty, old as the earth, and able to contain the full breadth of mystery I suspected existed in the world. After years of dreaming, I visited the stones with my family when I was in high school. Salisbury Plain was gray and windswept, and driving the highway across it I was surprised by how small the stones seemed. When we parked and crossed the street, I was appalled by the ropes cordoning off the tourists. How dare they! Finally my family dispersed and I, resigned to the well-worn paths, wandered in and out of the stones' shadows. Balanced atop one another against the blustering wind, the stones exerted a surprising silence. They felt closed off, as though hunkered inside themselves. I'd been hoping for exhilaration in this first meeting, or at least for a glimpse of their secret. Instead I felt quieted. Whatever sat in the circle's center that day remained inaccessible.

Stonehenge was sacred for me in part because of the cultural traditions surrounding it (the awe, the myths, the tourist attraction) and in part because of my personal relationship with it (a dreamy girl whose imagination was not fully sparked by Christianity). My meeting with the stones was holy, but not in the manner I had anticipated. The richness of my simple pilgrimage was elicited when the place (with its history, its legacy, its solid fact) came into contact with my being. Both place and self need their due on the page. Without the filter of my story, the reader has no access to the stones' presence nor their potential influence. Likewise, holy sites in your story must earn their holiness by your effort and example.

The corollary to this principle is that any ordinary place can be made holy by a writer's attention. "Earth's crammed with heaven," Elizabeth Barrett Browning writes, "And every common bush afire with God." You needn't seek out places of grandeur or notoriety, but rather simply sit, as Thich Nhat Hanh teaches, on "your own spot. It is on this very spot and in this very moment that you can become enlightened." Wherever you sit now is setting enough for a memoir.

I write these words in a small office with one blue wall and three white. The window over my desk faces east and looks through a screened porch and down my front sidewalk, which is shaded by a towering pine. Stacked to my right are my sacred texts—a dictionary, a thesaurus, the Bible, a notebook of quotations, and the last few years of journals. I'm comforted by their closeness. To my left is a framed photograph of the Hudson River, the view from my parents' back deck. In the photo trees stripe the foreground with vertical shadows; behind them the sky blazes orange and the water is a dull bronze. The slope and scoop of the hills on the other side are as familiar as my breath. This is where I create. The empty desk, the hardwood floors, and skyblue wall secure me in place so I may dive into the interior realm of unknowing.

Sharing Suffering

"THERE'S NO SUCH THING as a bad experience," a writing teacher reprimanded me once, shortly after I'd lost all my belongings in a fire. "There's only good material."

I was annoyed. But I sat down to write about the fire, and, sure enough, it made a great story. The fire was traumatic and my losses grievous; writing it out was equally painful. Memoirists live life twice, and this isn't always desirable. But there is something redemptive about making hardship into a story. Transforming bad experiences into good material doesn't ease the loss of nineteen years of journals and my mother's handmade quilt, nor does it stop the panic that still overtakes me every time I see large flames. All it does is hold the hardship within the container of a story. And this, strangely enough, is a restorative gift—both for the writer and the reader.

No spiritual memoir is worth its salt without a good look at darkness. Indeed, it is often loss or trauma that stirs up a spiritual journey and the corresponding need to write about it. When we dig down to the wellspring of our stories, we inevitably confront suffering, and suffering presents its own writing challenges. That traumatic experiences make good material is both good and bad news—at least something worthwhile emerges from our suffering, but we must live through it again on the page.

To write about darkness, we must look at it directly. Anne Sexton writes, "I think that writers must try not to avoid knowing what is happening. Everyone has somewhere the ability to mask the events of pain and sorrow. . . . But the creative person must not use this mechanism any more than they have to in order to keep breathing." Denial is natural. In the case of trauma, it is necessary for survival. But the integrity of the story demands that we cut through layers of denial to expose truth, including its factual and emotional attributes. Only the full ramifications of a difficult experience make a solid story.

When a writer avoids the story's hardships, the gaps are always blatant to the reader. It may be human nature to shy away from ugliness and pain and complexity, but secretly we are all curious about how others grapple with the darkness. Everyone seeks to resolve the conundrums that suffering presents in their lives. Especially in memoir, readers are unwilling to settle for platitudes or Pollyanna portrayals of difficult circumstances. Such falsities fail to address the core reason for reading—to find out how the author sorts through life's cruel paradoxes. Readers keep writers responsible by refusing to read on if a story is truncated in any way.

Truth-telling can be excruciating. "The greatest nonfiction writers," Bly writes, "are the ones who are willing to put up with extremely uncomfortable, miserable thoughts, for days and weeks and years on end." This is why self-care must become your first priority. Even if you've done a dozen years of therapy, performed healing rituals, and made peace with your agonizing story, writing it out brings memories to the fore again. Powerful emotions arise, as well as unwelcome insights and forgotten incidents.

The journey you take through the writing process can be heartrending, so it's important to honor your needs throughout. Go at a pace that is comfortable but also slightly challenging. Take breaks when the writing becomes unbearable. Don't give up. Reward yourself when you achieve small goals. Seek professional support if the writing evokes extreme responses, such as depression, panic attacks, or other signs of inner turmoil—all of which signal the power of your story. Treat your inner work—the time you spend responding with feeling to memories and adjusting to your discoveries—with grave respect. This inner work is integral to your writing, even if it seems like you're not producing anything.

Good self-care regarding a story's content also results in good reader care. Writers of trauma frequently ask how much their readers can bear. Why, they ask, would anyone subject themselves to the horrific events of my life? None of us would willingly choose unrelenting suffering. And yet suffering is universal and inevitable; our readers know it and are curious about how to survive it. Our propensity for rubbernecking at traffic accidents may not be voyeurism so much as survival instinct—we learn from the mishaps of others. Nevertheless, consideration of the reader's tolerance for hardship can be a good moderator for ourselves. We need humor, digression, hopefulness, and breathers from tragedy as much as the reader does.

What draws a reader through a story, regardless of its content, is not hope or happiness but movement. In the classic memoir *Night*, Wiesel's budding interest in Jewish mysticism is interrupted by the Nazi takeover. Wiesel loses his hometown, his boyhood, and his family to the Holocaust. By the end of the book he has seen absolute evil.

He understands death to be a form of freedom. God has vanished. Wiesel's story is plain, without gloss or humor; he exposes his readers to extreme human cruelty. But it is a gift nonetheless because it is true. The narrative's forward motion and the movement of Wiesel's soul toward despair keep us turning the pages.

At the beginning of *Bones of the Master*, George Crane tells of Tsung Tsai's journey out of inner Mongolia during the Chinese Cultural Revolution. Tsung Tsai, a Ch'an Buddhist monk, escaped religious persecution, traveled the width of his country by foot and by jumping railcars, and finally crawled under the fence into Hong Kong. The famine, illness, death, and physical hardship he endured during his escape were inordinate in their severity. But the reader knows from the start that Tsung Tsai is drinking tea with Crane; he survived. We're willing to witness his gruesome ordeal to learn how he survived. When humans endure terrific suffering, a degree of our affliction comes of not knowing if or when the suffering will end. But in any memoir, the reader receives assurance from page one: The narrator has survived to tell the tale.

Writers of crises often fear that they are wallowing in self-pity and alienating the reader. In the hundreds of manuscripts I've read, I haven't once come across a story in which the centerpiece is "Woe is me!" Most beginning writers err in the opposite direction, worrying that their hardships are burdensome; they therefore censor horror and pain to protect the reader. This is a form of literary codependence. Never take care of the reader by truncating your story. You can make a difficult story more entertaining, accessible, aesthetic, gripping, or graphic to keep the reader engaged. But never dishonor your story's depth with evasion.

Ultimately your memoir isn't about you. Your story is a means to explore the human experience and the life of the spirit. Shine the light through the details of your suffering to this core. "Aim for the chopping block," Annie Dillard writes. "If you aim for the wood, you will have nothing. Aim past the wood, aim through the wood; aim for the chopping block."

If shining the spotlight on hard memories is too difficult, there are techniques for peeking around the shadows and still getting at the truth. When Lisa Dietz, a woman I work with who writes about severe trauma, finds herself flinching or avoiding a scene, she then "writes in the negative space." Instead of describing the event itself, she describes the air temperature or the music playing in the background. In other words, she concentrates first on the details that surround the traumatic event. These are manageable and relatively harmless. Then Dietz infuses those details with the emotion of the moment. What she's discovered is that filling in the negative space leaves a distinct, positive image in the reader's mind. For example, a woman might describe the wallpaper she stared at while she was being raped, with its bizarrely isolated but comforting pink roses. The wallpaper tells a stronger story than the rape itself because it reveals how the woman is forced to abandon her body for the safer haven of two-dimensional rosebuds.

Had it been too traumatizing for me to write about the fifty-foot flames that lapped at all I owned, I could have described the Norwegian pines that cast shadows and loomed over the trembling group of witnesses. The details surrounding trauma contain the moment's weight. When you can't bear to hear from the event itself, let the details speak.

❧ Choose a memory that is emotionally loaded. Without ever addressing the event itself, write in the negative space. Describe the setting, the light, the sounds, people's clothing, etc. Note how the details tell much of the story for you.

Metaphor is also a gracious aid you can use to capture painful events. If it is too difficult to write about the emotions of a tragedy, you may be able to say what they were like. When Gretel Ehrlich was struck by lightning and horribly mistreated at the hospital, she sensed her life ebbing: "Death resided in the room: not as a human figure but as a dark fog rolling in, threatening to cover me." It's a natural impulse to reach outside the literal moment for a figurative analogy. Fear shadows us; anger enflames us; illness descends like humidity. Grief, to poet Denise Levertov, is "a homeless dog / who comes to the back door / for a crust, for a meatless bone." Scott Russell Sanders' early encounter with mortality leads him to realize "I was temporary, a loose knot that would come untied." Margaret Wurtele writes about the death of her son on a mountain rescue mission in *Touching the Edge*. She wonders how to reconcile loss with the continued existence of good:

> I lay in bed that night, feeling suspended, as if I were weight-less, floating alone in space. Here I was, in the middle of my life. On the one hand, everything was falling apart. My only son was dead, my best friend was dying. I was scared, angry, and confused. . . . On the other hand, I had received the prom-ise of new life: being Maxwell's godmother, the possibility that Heidi and Caley might marry some day and give us a grandchild. . . . As I lay there, I became aware that deep, deep inside of me was an untouchable core, a precious inner sanc-

turn that was insulated from all these things happening around me, both the bad and the good. That center seemed to burn like a pilot light, a constant, dependable source of energy whose flame held steady no matter what happened on the outside. Was that ineffable center in the depths of my being a connection to everything else, my link to a unity in which I participated? Could I learn to tune in to that place more regularly, to rely on its steady flame in the face of the unpredictable swirl of life around me?

We instinctively grasp for images—fog, a dog, a pilot light—to help us comprehend incomprehensible suffering.

❧ Recall a moment of intense grief, physical pain, or trauma. Be in that moment and look out at the world through its lens. What do you see? What landscape, object, animal, or room? Describe something outside of yourself through the lens of your feeling. Compare this with a moment of happiness. How do the different emotions affect what and how you observe?

You can also write about difficult memories by thoroughly establishing the context. When beginning writers have been touched by a grave loss and are inspired to write about it, they have a tendency to assume that the story resides in the loss itself. For example, if a man wants to write about his mother's death, he begins by describing her stroke and physical decline, or if a woman wants to write about her stay in the psychiatric ward, she starts with her breakdown. These are certainly the hearts of their stories and will have a central place in their memoirs. But the weight of any loss is gathered prior to the moment of loss. The mother's death has import only as much as her life has intersected with the writer's, and the decline of mental health can only be appreciated in the context of the writer's dreams and well-being.

Here is an example. Say your dog Skipper was run over by a car, and you want to write his story. If you begin with that fateful morning, describing the screech of brakes and awful thump, and proceed to tell of your wrenching grief, you may elicit some sympathy from your reader and honor the impact of your loss. But you have not honored Skipper, nor your relationship. If you take time during your story to describe how, while Skipper was alive, he could intuit your moods, how your tears brought him loping to your lap, how pitiful and trusting his eyes were after he broke his leg, and how he slept at the foot of your bed for twelve years, you make the substance of the story the substance of your loss. You honor Skipper's life and your grief. Not only that— chances are that your reader will have a visceral response when you describe Skipper's ignoble death. By fleshing out a portrait of Skipper and of your relationship, you give the reader an opportunity to grow attached to him. When the car crash ends Skipper's life, the reader is more apt to grieve with you, feeling the full extent of your loss.

   Return in your thoughts to a moment of vulnerability as a child. Write that memory; then explore what it teaches you about your childhood beliefs. Early encounters with death, even the death of a pet, reveal our childhood perceptions and questions of spirit. Moments of crisis in childhood expose our early beliefs.

Every loss has a history that gives it gravity, and this history is essential to the story. Thus a good deal of background writing is necessary to support stories of tragedy. For writers struggling with difficult material, this is good news. Your experience of wholeness reveals your hurt, so you must write about the good moments too. When writers want to accent the qualities of their main characters, they often create a *foil*, a side character with contrasting qualities (Shakespeare's assured Laertes highlights Hamlet's indecision, and Jane Austen's gentle Jane Bennet underscores Elizabeth's strong will in *Pride and Prejudice*). Memories of connection and health serve as foils for those memories of brokenness. A student of mine was having trouble writing about her mother's emotional vacuity until she remembered her grandmother, who nurtured her and taught her about attentive listening. The writer knew her mother's lack only because she had experienced her grandmother's fullness. Writing about both accentuated the difference. A Catholic priest wanted to write the story of leaving the church because he was unwilling to be celibate; he began with his fond, formative memories of seminary, thereby making the loss more poignant. Our sadness is bound inextricably with our joy. Only together can they make our stories complete.

If you have reached healing or resolution in relation to your loss, this too is an essential part of the story. A wise, whole narrator provides a distanced perspective; the reader relies on this voice as evidence that difficult scenes will end and learning will emerge. Drop hints of how far you've come in relationship to your suffering (at the story's beginning and as it unfolds) to make the reader curious enough to plow through painful passages. The reader wants to know the consequences of suffering and how you integrate them into life's broader scope. The "after" portion of your story is as essential as "before" and "during." Having experienced hardship with you, the reader is now more tolerant of (and perhaps even eager for) your pearls of wisdom.

It's not necessary to achieve recovery in order to write about loss. Doty wrote about Wally's deterioration and his own subsequent grief as it was happening. A student of mine wrote her way through an incarceration; she tapped her notebooks from this period for their wealth of detail as she put together her memoir. The writing you produce when you are in pain is raw and can have an energy that is impossible to achieve after the fact.

However, in the midst of suffering it is difficult to discern meaning, give it form, or bring your narrative to completion. Time and healing provide the perspective needed to know the full ramifications of what has happened. By all means, write through the rawness, but then allow your writing to mature just as you do. What makes a story whole is not necessarily the healing of your brokenness or any philosophical revelation about suffering; what makes it whole is movement, from one way of being toward another, and balance.

    Think of a moment of intense grief that you have come to peace with or that you feel comfortable writing about. Write the story with particular attention to your experience of grief. What was it like? (Remember to check in with your body.) Then move ahead to the point in time when your grief met transformation, some easing of pain occurred, or you achieved a reconciliation with the loss. What happened then? Tell that story, too.

Stories that accurately portray spiritual darkness are a great gift. So much of spiritual writing is sugarcoated; spirituality, many people assume, is synonymous with happiness. This delusion does injustice to the central role death, doubt, and despair play in spiritual formation. Our personal shortcomings and the horrifying faults of humanity (violence, oppression, betrayal, anger, malice) must be accounted for in our spiritual world view. Even holiness has a shadow side, which we experience as emptiness or silence and cannot deny if our stories are to have integrity. It's this very integrity that is our reward. At the end of a difficult story, we can take comfort in our loyalty to experience and in our witness to the truth.

The Numinous

WHEN I WAS QUITE YOUNG I dreamt I was in a room with a bank of windows facing a lake. Around the room were scattered pieces of wooden machinery. A man told me it was time for me to die; how would I like this to happen? That's when I realized the machines were implements of torture. I walked down to the still water, sat on a log, and pondered my choices. Fire, I decided; I would die by fire. Back in the house, the man put me in a closet filled waist-high with loose, blank sheets of paper. They rustled around me lightly, like moths' wings. Then he lit a match.

Twenty-five years and a traumatic fire later, I'm still haunted by the calmness with which I made that dream decision. Burning is a horrible way to die. But dreams exaggerate, and this one disclosed a truth about my life that becomes increasingly clear every year: I must always choose my passion, whatever the danger. And my passion invariably involves reams of paper. Writing is the means, not the end.

For many spiritual seekers the archetypal, illogical, and luminous realm of mysticism plays a heavy hand in our journeys. The dead visit, God speaks, kundalini energy ignites our core, and dreams steer our choices. The ineffable world on "the other side of the veil" slips through the cracks of consciousness and leaves us stammering, speechless. Often decades pass before we integrate such experiences, and we rarely if ever comprehend their full import. Even my childhood dream, for all its simplicity, has a force that still unveils itself. How, then, can we write about the numinous? How can we do justice to dreams, visions, and mystical experiences with that inept tool that is language?

    What is the earliest night dream you can remember? Write it out in detail. Describe how you have interpreted this dream over the years, remaining aware that multiple interpretations can coexist comfortably. In what ways has this dream described your life? Informed it?

DREAMS AS TEACHERS

Roseann Guigere, a Sister of St. Joseph and a mentor of mine, describes the dreams we have at night as our most intimate form of scripture. Every dream is a story uniquely crafted for you and no other; each dream, no matter how disturbing, works for your healing. "In our sleep," the ancient poet Aeschylus writes, "pain that cannot forget falls drop by drop upon the heart / And in our own despair, against our will, comes wisdom through the awful grace of God." Night dreams are perhaps our most common and accessible encounters with the numinous. As such, they can teach us much about writing other, more complex experiences. The guidelines for writing dreams that follow apply as well to larger, odder mystical encounters.

It's always good to write dreams down immediately; they are like quicksilver and will slither from under the hand of consciousness.

Write dreams in present tense, as they always happen in the now. Writing in present tense places you more fully in the scene, where you're apt to remember more details. The initial record of a dream is about preservation, not art. All the dimensions and ramifications of even a straightforward dream will not be immediately obvious. The passage of time allows the bud of a dream to bloom. But recording dreams immediately helps you capture their newness, and the writing process may steady your foothold in reality. Write at first without any thought of your audience; write for the sheer sake of recording or digesting the experience. Later on, as you begin to craft your memoir, you'll be grateful for the details.

Even a piece of a dream is worth honoring. Dreams are like holograms: The whole is contained in each fragment. While you might lose sight of the complete narrative, a single image or word from a dream can hold its emotional message. Besides, the entirety of most dreams or visions is incomprehensible, while small parts are more likely to make themselves understood.

> ❧ *Consider an image from a night dream, daydream, or vision that haunts you. Describe it in detail. Then converse with it. What does it have to say to you? What do you have to say to it? What difference does it make that this image is in your life?*

It's rare that anyone has a handle on a dream's meaning right away. The more numinous the dream, the more time it takes for its significance to be revealed. For this reason, allow yourself plenty of time to journal about a dream. Give it a title. Dialogue with its striking images. Allow months—or years, even—for potent dreams to yield their full import before writing about them in a public way. Time sorts the chaff from the wheat; it gives dreams their proportional place in your broader story.

Whether or not you intend to include excerpts from dreams in your memoir, developing a habit of working with your dreams can teach a lot about how metaphor functions and how to tell a story with multiple layers of meaning. When a moose appears in your dream, you might assume it's there because your brother told a joke about a moose the night before. Later, you remember the Boundary Waters trip when you watched a moose swim across the lake and felt a pang for that huge, creaturely freedom. Browsing in a magazine, you learn that moose can swim to the bottom of lakes. Over time your dream image grows multidimensional. The lumbering animal is a messenger from the depths, an invitation to be wild, a joke the Great Trickster tells to get your attention. If you work to articulate the facets you understand and to uncover those you don't, you gain increasing appreciation for imagery and its natural resonance. It becomes easier to recognize which images from your memory are worth milking for their full strength. Every literary analogy is a mere shadow of the dream world's power because the true master of metaphor is the human psyche.

WRITING VISIONS

One time a student handed me a thirty-page manuscript of visions he had received over an intense two-year period of solitude. The visions were extraordinary—multicolored, moving between the past and future, packed with astute messages and unfathomable symbols. Page after page, these visions jumped from human hunger for knowledge to utopian images of community to demanding messages from the animal world. I was both fascinated and bored stiff.

I was fascinated because this student had a remarkable gift and was certainly more receptive to the spirit world than I will ever be. I was bored because the visions, without context or consequence, lacked roots in real life. They floated just beyond my grasp. I couldn't figure out why they might matter to me. The author had assumed the visions themselves had inherent value and had eliminated as much of himself from the writing as possible. This, he thought, would keep them pure. They would speak directly to the reader.

I had to break the news that he had assumed incorrectly. When we are swept away in the bizarre otherworldliness of a visionary or mystical experience, it's easy to lose sight of all we've learned about writing well (establish a setting, develop characters, describe the before and after to give context, link the ineffable to the concrete, etc.). These principles still apply, however ethereal our story. The reader needs shoes to walk around in, a place to feel at home, thought patterns to follow, and stimulated senses. If anything, the reader needs *more* grounding when the subject matter is otherworldly; otherwise we risk our reader's disbelief. Besides, mystical experiences become significant only when translated into the stuff of the daily round; they gain communal relevance only when they inform relationships and institutions. "What fruit dost thou bring back from this thy vision?" is the final question Jacopone da Todi asks of the mystic. This integration comprises the fundamental story of mysticism, reconnecting the Great Beyond back to the here and now.

     Consider a dream, vision, or mystical experience that has played a large role in your spiritual life. Draw a time line and place your experience at the halfway mark. List the preceding events that informed your experience and the consequences of that moment. The time line is a quick sketch of your context. If you wish, write the time-line events into stories.

One of the strongest teachers for grappling with visions is Black Elk, whose memoir was told orally in the 1930s to John Neihardt, a Nebraskan poet, and published as *Black Elk Speaks*. Black Elk, a Lakota tribal leader and medicine man, had his great vision during an illness when he was nine years old:

> Then I was standing on the highest mountain of them all, and round about beneath me was the whole hoop of the world. And while I stood there I saw more than I can tell and I understood more than I saw; for I was seeing in a sacred manner the shapes of all things in the spirit, and the shape of all shapes as they must live together like one being. And I saw that the sacred hoop of my people was one of many hoops that made one circle, wide as daylight and as starlight, and in the center grew one mighty flowering tree to shelter all the children of one mother and one father. And I saw that it was holy.

After twelve days, when Black Elk returned to consciousness, he was clueless about how to respond to so potent a vision:

> As I lay there thinking about the wonderful place where I had been and all that I had seen, I was very sad; for it seemed to me that everybody ought to know about it, but I was afraid to tell, because I knew that nobody would believe me, little as I was, for I was only nine years old. Also, as I lay there thinking

of my vision, I could see it all again and feel the meaning with a part of me like a strange power glowing in my body; but when the part of me that talks would try to make words for the meaning, it would be like fog and get away from me.

Black Elk's transition back to boyhood was rough; he was "homesick" for the place where he had been. Black Elk held his vision secret until he was sixteen, when he was overtaken by an inexplicable fear and heard many voices telling him, "It is time!" Finally, with the help of a medicine man, he was able to perform his vision in the Horse Dance for the whole community to witness. "A man who has a vision is not able to use the power of it until after he has performed the vision on earth for the people to see," he tells us. Gradually, as Black Elk disclosed his vision to his people through ceremony, the vision's power manifested itself in his tribal leadership and ability to heal. The vision also perplexed him as the white settlers betrayed and destroyed his people. Toward the end of his life, when he shared his story with Neihardt, Black Elk was profoundly disturbed that the tree of his people remained withered and dead rather than thriving, as he'd foreseen.

Black Elk Speaks models honest portrayal of a mystical experience. It begins with the context of Black Elk's childhood. It describes the vision in detail and then shows its full ramifications—Black Elk's confusion and isolation, how the vision was both burden and inspiration, and how it affected Black Elk's actions. The majority of the story is taken up by the intersection between the vision and the reality of the white settlers' betrayal and displacement of the Lakota people. Rather than distracting us from the vision, this context reveals the vision as a dynamic agent throughout Black Elk's life. The context gives the vision significance.

♌ Consider a significant mystical experience you've had, preferably in your distant past. Identify another memory that illustrates how this experience shifted your behavior, belief, or thought. Write both stories, conveying both the mystical experience and its long-term impact.

RESISTANCE AND SKEPTICISM

When bizarre, inexplicable things happen along the spiritual journey, it's a rare traveler who takes them in stride. Most of us trip up mightily over mystical encounters. It's a joke among spiritual directors that a person's biggest obstacle to experiencing God is his or her last experience of God. A healthy dose of fear and denial is human; it keeps us answerable to reality and protects us from too much holiness. On the other hand, extreme resistance undercuts the impact of mystical experiences. Mystics walk a precarious road.

When it comes to writing, particularly within this scientifically oriented society, your initial resistance to a mystical experience is not something to be ashamed of, not evidence of small faith, but rather a response with which the reader is likely to identify. Skepticism becomes a means for the skeptical reader to participate in your story. Kim Chernin's *In My Father's Garden* is a good example of how skepticism can provide common ground for the author and the reader. Chernin is a feminist, psychoanalyst, and declared "unbeliever"; her parents were active communists and raised Chernin as an atheist. But when Chernin sits with a client's dying mother and finds her hands "heating up with an intensity that seems to stream out," this healing energy overturns all she assumes about the world:

Because I am afraid of my thoughts I try to keep myself from thinking. Cloud patches of the not-quite-thought cross the space I am trying to keep empty. I remember the family story about my grandmother and her healing hands. . . . My own hands have always been useless, dropping things, unable to thread needles, tie knots. Now these hands have become knowing, autonomous, indifferent to my confusion. They have found their work, they are getting on with it.

Chernin's discomfort with this inexplicable sensation gives the reader permission to be uncomfortable as well. As much as I like the *idea* of hands strangely and palpably radiating energy, the *fact* makes me squirm. Most of us would prefer nature to be predictable. That Chernin is equally thrown off balance makes her story more believable. She tussles with paradox—evidence of a true spiritual struggle.

    ❧ *Choose a small, unusual experience of spirit that you cannot rationally explain. Write the story, attending to the details. Describe any doubts, either from the time of the experience or from the present, without worrying about what the reader might think.*

Your own skepticism, doubt, fear, and denial are an essential part of your story. They are the foil for ecstasy, the shadow that helps the reader recognize the light. Likewise, the despair and disorientation that often follow profound events are integral to the whole story, as in Robert Johnson's *Balancing Heaven and Earth*:

After thirty minutes of ecstasy on the mountainside that morning, I spent the next ten years in terrible suffering—not physical suffering, but the subtle hell of loneliness and isolation. I was doing all the standard things in life, but they meant very little to me. My visions came close to destroying the practicality in me, the usual human dimensions of existence. . . . I can't tell you how many times after that morning when I tasted heaven that I went to some high place to watch the sunrise again, hoping to hear the morning stars singing together as they had done at that glorious dawn. I yearned desperately to get a glimpse of that world. Everywhere I went I would find myself looking over the horizon or peering into someone's eyes, hoping to find it. Sometimes I would see just enough of it to tease me and make me feel worse.

Be straightforward about every emotional response to your brush with mystery. The full ramifications of your spiritual experiences teach the real consequences of mysticism.

When Black Elk performed his vision in ceremony, he was able to create a public bridge between the spirit world, as it was revealed to him, and his people. When contemporary writers set out to disclose our mystical experiences, we hope to create a similar bridge. Writing is one of the few ways modern people have to incorporate the power of our visions into our being; it is, perhaps, our way of "performing the vision on earth." Black Elk's Lakota community literally dressed as the horses, grandfathers, and thunder beings of his vision; they danced in the vision's movement and spoke the vision's messages. If memoirists can write about numinous encounters with attention and accuracy, if we present ordinary lives as a context and container for the extraordinary, if we humble ourselves at the limits of our understanding and yet continue to search, we invite the wider world to participate in the dance.

THE CRAFT OF WRITING

The meaning of the world is made, not found.
—DAVID BAYLES AND TED ORLAND

The Power of Showing, The Power of Telling

A YEAR AFTER my infant nephew died of Sudden Infant Death Syndrome—a loss that left me locked and breathless—I found myself reaching for books on grief and discovered Alla Renee Bozarth's classic *Life Is Goodbye, Life Is Hello*. Bozarth, an Episcopalian priest, first published her advice on grieving well in 1982, and gave this as a qualifier in her introduction: "Though I do not share the details of [my personal grief] journeys except for their lessons and gifts, or occasionally as one story in the context of many co-travelers' stories, I come to you in this book on the basis of what I have learned personally in my soul about letting go." Her book is instructive, steering readers through the various stages of grief. I was able to understand my initial numbness, my rage, my deep-seated emptiness at the loss of my nephew's life. In the first edition of her book, Bozarth chooses to withhold the stories of her own losses from the reader, creating an emotional distance and allowing her to be the authority on grief. As a result *Life Is Goodbye* has helped thousands of people better understand the grieving process.

The copy I read, however, had been republished in 1986 with an epilogue that Bozarth wrote shortly after losing her thirty-seven-year-old husband and soul mate of fifteen years. In the epilogue she chooses to lay her story bare: "Even now the waves of grief come over me, and I am stuck in a spasm, unable to move from unbearable intensity into release." Her writing is raw, honest, wrenching. For the two hundred pages of her "how to" instruction, my heart hurt but my eyes remained dry. Then I read this passage:

> One afternoon while I was having a massage and doing emotional work to release memories and grief from my muscles, something most unusual happened. When my massage therapist stroked the sole of my left foot, I sat bolt upright, stiffened, and stopped breathing. Neither of us was afraid, but in a few seconds Nancy said, "Alla, please breathe." I answered, "I don't want to." But I knew I was supposed to, and I obeyed, with shrieking sobs that left me shaking and trembling all over for a long time. Nancy held me until I was quite finished.

The severity of Bozarth's loss pierced through to my own, and I wept for the baby boy who would never grow up to call me aunt. Bozarth's story, for all its plainness, touched me in a way her instructive writing could not. It showed her grieving well and allowed me to do the same.

What is significant about Bozarth's epilogue is how she foregoes her distant voice of authority (the expert on grief) for a different kind of authority entirely—one rooted in a chaotic, unresolved experience. Suddenly she is walking beside me, as overcome by sorrow and as desperate for comfort. While her instructive writing conveys important information, it is her story that digs down and touches gold. Instructive writing speaks to the head, while story works on the heart. Until I read the epilogue I trusted Bozarth as a scholar. Afterward, I trusted her as a compatriot in loss.

It takes courage to crack open your story. I admire how Bozarth is willing to admit that she doesn't have all the answers—that, in the face of her husband's death, she is as mystified and inconsolable as the rest of us. For a grief expert this is a big risk. But it would be a risk for any writer, regardless of reputation, to launch into a true story without knowing precisely what it has to teach or why it must be written. This requires courage. Instead of simply passing on the wisdom culled from experience, allow yourself to launch into the unresolved mystery of what happened or is happening and flail about in the open. By flailing you increase the likelihood of learning something yourself. Bozarth's epilogue is powerful because the reader witnesses her moving through grief, not just talking about it afterward.

How can writers crack open stories so the raw experience is made available to readers, as well as to ourselves? Essentially it's a matter of showing rather than telling—the tried and true maxim of writing teachers. A scene is more powerful than a summary. I can tell you about the months in college when I questioned God's existence and floundered through my classes, doubtful of their worth if life had so little meaning. Or I can show you a night when I walked across campus, the lawns damp, and the black sky extending endlessly over the prairie. I felt the emptiness of space press on me like a heavy shadow. Precise constellations were scattered through the heavens, but I only saw the void, emptiness extending an unimaginable distance, and myself less than a speck. Without my childhood faith in a creator, despair reeled in me, flinging its darkness into every recess of my body. I walked across that field of hopelessness, unable to cry.

When we show in our writing, we create a scene. We linger on details. We paint a picture. We get inside the mind and body of our former self, and let the reader know what was going on in there. As much as possible, we reconstruct our memory so that the reader sees the sky we saw, tastes the bile on our tongue, quivers at the dampness of the grass, and hears our soul's inner grinding. How the sky looked the night I doubted God's existence isn't particularly relevant. And yet the lens through which I saw the sky—lonely, despairing—taints the image of the stars. I cannot describe the sky without also depicting my internal state. In this way, seemingly irrelevant details actually reveal the heart of a memory more accurately than the story itself.

The distinction between telling and showing is subtle and worth exploring. First, here's an example of telling that summarizes action:

> On an afternoon walk in Tokyo, I ran into the sweet potato vendor who changed my life.

To *show* what happens in this this story, I must make it into a scene:

> Tokyo was bustling that afternoon. I clipped my stride to accommodate the sidewalk crowds, but not enough—rounding a corner in the Ginza, I ran smack into a bent-over gentleman. He was pushing a snack cart, hawking sweet potatoes. Before I had time to apologize, our eyes met in shocking and intimate connection.

Note how showing uses images and movements. Beginning writers often abbreviate their stories by skipping these narrative elements, which are essential to making memoir come alive.

Beginning writers also tend to abridge conversation, as in this second example:

I explained to Mama that I didn't do it. Peter had set me up to look bad.

Compare this with the livelier:

"But Mama!" I whined. "I didn't do it. Peter gave me the knife, I swear!"

Dialogue makes the scene immediate.

A third manner of showing moves the reader below the surface of a character:

I grieved for months after my grandmother died. I suffered from insomnia and spent nights roaming her house, touching her things.

The action of this scene lurks in the thoughts and feelings of the narrator, so the more I highlight these, the more I am showing:

For months after my grandmother died, I was unable to sleep. I writhed in the bedsheets for hours, recollecting all the moments I might have expressed my love for her. Finally I rose and meandered through the dark house like a ghost, laying my hand on her polished tabletop, china lamp, kitchen counter. Their cool, solid presence made her seem all the more unreachable.

By entering the mind and heart of the narrator, the reader more fully inhabits the scene.

✍ *Find a photograph from your past. Describe the photograph in detail as an object in its own right. What observations can you make about your personality, your struggles, or your beliefs based on this image? Write them out in a straightforward, reflective voice. Then go back and rewrite the description. Can you reveal your insights through the details?*

The essence of spiritual experience is indescribable, but the material world is infused with meaning and is ultimately describable. Events burn their emotional import into our memories of ordinary objects, places, and people. One of my students describes how he play-acted the part of a priest using Ritz crackers and grape drink as a child. He memorized the mass and intoned it for his little brothers and sisters. His description of meticulously setting the cardboard box altar reveals a connection between his nine-year-old self and his God that no direct theological language can touch.

Dillard is masterful at using the material to point to the spiritual: "The weasel was stunned into stillness as he was emerging from beneath an enormous shaggy wild rose bush four feet away. I was stunned into stillness twisted backward on the tree trunk. Our eyes locked, and someone threw away the key." Dillard looks intently at the weasel, "ten inches long, thin as a curve, a muscled ribbon, brown as fruitwood, soft-furred, alert," and considers the weasel's instinct to bite its prey at the neck. In this instinct she finds a mandate to "grasp your one necessity and not let it go." Dillard's swift encounter with this creature is infused with her beliefs about her own animal instinct and capacity for passion. She describes the concrete to access the abstract.

The soul's nature is elusive; if we seek it head on, shining our flashlight directly at it, the soul flees. The soul is best discovered with peripheral vision; it thrives in the shadows. Spiritual writing is evi-

dence of the soul's nature; it deflates when we describe holiness directly and throbs with vivacity when we scribble along the edges.

    ୬ *Write a grocery list. Reflect on these needs. How are they*
particular to you? What do they say about nourishment? About
what feeds you? In what way are these needs fundamental to all
humans?

DETAILS, DETAILS

The phrase "God is in the details" gets bantered about in spiritual circles,
reminding us that nooks and crannies are fine places to find the sacred.
Whatever it is that gives writing spark and breath resides in the particular, the minute, the mundane. On the page, the words that are most likely to embody our experiences are solid words—nouns we can see, smell,
and touch; verbs we feel in our muscles; adjectives that surprise and par-
ticularize. If we wish our writing to be not just about the spiritual but to
actually *contain* the spiritual—to hold the potential for connection and
transformation for readers—then we must attend to the details.

    ୬ *Without looking, conjure up the image of a photograph*
from your past. Write your memory of that moment. Then
examine the photograph, paying acute attention to the details
(the light, your clothing, the objects that surround you). Rewrite
the memory including these details.

In general, beginning writers fall into two categories: *overwriters*
and *underwriters*. Overwriters are the rarer breed; they produce vast
amounts of material, digress widely from their subject, and use an

overabundance of detail. Often they are unafraid to use their voice; they revel in filling reams of paper. First drafts come swiftly. Some overwriters presume an interested audience and have no qualms about taking up space. Other overwriters are insecure about the clarity of their voice and believe they cannot communicate effectively without explaining their subject to death. They cushion their stories with qualifications and unnecessary details.

Far more common are the underwriters, who can't imagine anyone wanting to read their story. These humble people put down mere skeletons of ideas, avoiding the details for fear that they will bore the reader. Underwriters summarize conversations rather than using dialogue. They rush to the conclusion, which is often abstract and incomprehensible, because they figure the reader is eager to get to the point. Underwriters are in a great hurry. They feel self-conscious about putting themselves at center stage.

Overwriters and underwriters need each others' gifts. The overwriter's task in revision is to pare down, to find the essential matter and let go of the rest. The underwriter's task is to put some meat on those bones. Both need to discern which moments in the story have emotional import and deserve to be stretched out in all their glory. Scenes with extraneous detail are aimless, and scenes without any detail are flat. But details that broaden the story, reveal the characters, or help ground the reader in a scene are never dull.

The question I often ask myself as I'm writing is, What details are doing the work of this piece? In the description of my Godless night at college, I don't include what I was wearing because my clothing, in this instance, reveals nothing about my state of mind. I do portray the damp grass because it mirrors the cold I felt inside, and I describe the wide prairie sky because I felt small in that moment, and my description of the heavens accents this. Were I to revise this paragraph, I might also include the looming facades of the academic buildings surrounding me. The sharp disciplines of academia spurred my doubt and formed the backdrop for my questioning, so this detail may give context to the scene. If the scene's purpose is to capture how doubt sapped the purpose from my life, then I can describe the empty night sky for far longer than in the example and still hold the reader's attention. These details do the work of the piece.

I call this *stretching the moment*. When a scene is central to the story, linger on the details that reveal its significance. A friend of mine refers to this technique as "building a Dagwood sandwich"; she takes the two slices of bread (the beginning and end of a scene) and packs more meaty, cheesy layers (the details) between them, taking care that the sandwich doesn't grow too big to eat. The details are what give a significant scene substance.

> ⤮ *Identify a scene that is important to your story. If you are an underwriter, stretch the moment by lingering on as many telling details as you can recall. If you are an overwriter, identify and linger on the telling details; then cut all other extraneous prose.*

Attending to the details is a way of listening for what our memories have to teach us. It's a manner of paying attention—a profoundly spiritual discipline that all creative writers practice. Details, particularly sensory details, are also how authors give our experiences to the reader. Take, for example, this passage from "Eating Dirt." Brian Doyle watches his two-year-old twins in the garden:

The boys are eating so much dirt so fast that much of it is missing their maws and sliding down their chicken chests. It is thick, moist dirt, slightly more solid than liquid. I watch a handful as it travels toward the sun. It's rich brown stuff, almost black, crumbly. There are a couple of tiny pebbles, the thin lacy bones of a former leaf (hawthorn?), the end of a worm, the tiny green elbows of bean sprouts. I watch with interest as Son Two inserts the dirt, chews meditatively, emits the wriggling worm, stares at it—and eats it again.

Doyle's dirt is so animated, so meticulously described, that we can feel it, smell it, and even taste it. Our imaginations project us into the scene; we're not passive bystanders. And we react strongly: Why doesn't he stop them?

Doyle goes on to explore how we're all made of dirt; dirt is an element uniting us with all creation. "Grizzled dirt leans against a fence . . . and watches dirt demons devour dirt, and the world spins in its miraculous mysterious circles, dust unto dust." After the image of his sons shoveling dirt down their throats, we'll never forget how dirt composes us.

Humans are bodily creatures; we need the contours of a landscape to feel grounded, the wrinkles on a man's face to imagine his smile, the reverberation of a bell to know its ritualistic import. When you write down these details you not only discover holiness, you also give the discovery of holiness to your readers. Or you give the reader despair at the absence of holiness or the ache for purpose in time's ruthless progression. In the end, all you have are fragments of sensory experience— conversations that haunt you, morning thunderstorms that hold you in your warm home, an occasional moment when ease swells in your chest like a bud. The details invite you—and the reader—inside, where the essence of matter resides.

When Telling Works

Having just sung the praises of showing over telling, I need to muddy the waters. While memoirs are propelled forward and organized by narrative, they also have an enormous capacity for the reflective voice—for ruminating, making meaning, drawing connections, and asking questions. That's why it's often hard to distinguish between memoir and personal essay, a form driven by ideas. Spiritual memoirists especially have a tendency to step aside from their stories to bind the content of their lives to a theology or to a larger spiritual framework. This may well be a legacy of Augustine, who veered from life events into preaching with seamless ease:

> The tumult within my breast hurried me out into [the garden], where no one would stop the raging combat that I had entered into against myself. . . . I suffered from a madness that was to bring health, and I was in a death agony that was to bring life: for I knew what a thing of evil I was, but I did not know the good that I would be after but a little while . . . . For all my bones cried out to me to enter into that covenant [with God], and by their praises they lifted me up into the skies. Not by ships, or in chariots, or on foot do we enter therein; we need not go even so far as I had gone from the house to the place where we were sitting.

While we may take issue with Augustine's beliefs, we have to admire how effortlessly he weaves his broader understanding of the sacred with the particulars of his personal story. This is challenging work.

Augustine's overt, didactic tone doesn't sit well with modern readers; we grow uncomfortable whenever a writer presumes to know which ultimate truths ought to be hammered into our skulls. But it is still possible to put forward what we believe (or to simply ponder mysteries) in an inviting, engaging manner, as the following examples from contemporary memoirs show. The first is from *Dreams of Trespass*, a memoir by Fatima Mernissi about her childhood growing up in a domestic harem in Morocco. In this passage, Mernissi is nine years old and attending the hadra, a ritual of dancing where the women are possessed by willful spirits. She watches Mina, a member of her household and a former slave:

> Mina danced slowly with her head swaying just slightly from right to left and her body erect. She only reacted to the softest of the rhythms, and even then, she danced off of the beat, as if the music she was dancing to was coming from inside. I admired her for that and for a reason I still do not understand. Maybe it was because I always enjoyed slow motion, and dreamed of life as a quiet and unhurried dance. Or maybe it was because Mina managed to combine two seemingly contradictory roles—to dance with a group, but also to keep her own offbeat rhythm. I wanted to dance like her, with the community, but also to my own secret music, springing from a mysterious source deep within, and stronger than the drums. Once I asked Mina why she danced so smoothly while most of the other women made abrupt, jerky movements,

and she said that many of the women confused liberation with agitation. "Some ladies are angry with their lives," she said, "and so even their dance becomes an expression of that." Angry women are hostages of their anger. They cannot escape it and set themselves free, which is indeed a sad fate. The worst of prisons is the self-created one.

The theme of captivity runs throughout Mernissi's memoir, since she was confined most days within the walls of her family's harem. Her journey is toward the liberation of her spirit inside this captivity. Notice how Mernissi first shows the dance, and how Mina's independent, slow movements appeal to her as a child. As readers, we feel Mina's freedom before we hear Mernissi's explanation. When she writes, "Angry women are hostages of their anger," we picture the other women's jerky, frustrated dancing; we connect an image to an idea, thereby making the idea more accessible and digestible: It is possible to be imprisoned externally and maintain one's internal freedom. By the time Mernissi uses her telling voice, the reader has already arrived at the same conclusion. Mernissi articulates what is underneath the story, tying its meaning to her broader purpose.

   Practice writing a conclusive statement at the end of a scene or story in your memoir. If it feels didactic, moralistic, or summative, that's all right—you're just training yourself to probe for the story's gist.

This order—first show, then tell—is by no means a hard-and-fast rule. But it is an effective technique. If you want to give your experience to the reader, this order is a more accurate representation; generally experience informs thought and not the other way around. Many beginning writers present insights up front, as though justifying the story that follows. Starting with a topic sentence is a technique impressed upon us so relentlessly by English teachers that it's a hard habit to break. In memoir, as in any storytelling, prefacing the story with its lesson is largely unnecessary and often has the effect of stealing the discovery away from the reader.

When you show first, you may find that telling is unnecessary. How marvelous! Stories make a point graphically and therefore more effectively than overt reflection. If your story accomplishes this, there is no need to repeat yourself by telling. Trust the story to do the work for you.

> ✍ *Return to the conclusive statement you wrote for the preceding exercise and cut it from your story. Can you show this conclusion within the story, rather than telling it? Rewrite the passage to incorporate your concluding insight.*

Reflective writing can help you focus your story. What makes a memoir work is a big search. Direct language that articulates that search can be stimulating and clarifying. It is good practice to write out the questions that drive you to write, as this crystallizes your quest on the page. If it feels natural, you can include these questions within the story itself to guide your reader.

Memoirs that lean toward the personal essay form are instructive in how they steer the story with overt reflection. Take, for example, "Waiting for a Miracle: A Jew Goes Fishing," by Marjorie Sandor. She begins with a memory of fishing in the Colorado River one Saturday morning. Looking up to the bridge above her, she sees "a dozen Hasids in long black coats and fedoras . . . gazing down at me, mournfully stroking their beards." Sandor knows herself judged: "What kind of chutzpah was this, a Jew trying to walk in harmony with nature? And in the water, no less, that famous Christian element." This encounter gets Sandor wondering whether there is a prohibition against fishing on the Sabbath and why those pious Jews are themselves out gazing at the water. "Surely they'd come further than any fisherman to stand on the bank of this river, which now, under a passing cloud, turned that promising greeny-gray that says *trout* to some people, and in so doing, says something about the mysteries we all wait for: Divine before you see it, mortal when you do."

Note how Sandor immediately establishes a scene. It is brief, without much of a plot. But the frowns of those men explain her subsequent foray into Jewish lore and into her personal history. She gives an experiential reason for her reflections; a visual image to latch on to as she moves into more abstract territory. This not only draws the reader into the story, it also grounds Sandor's reflections in a real event. Questions arise as a natural consequence of the scene.

Note also that when Sandor asks a question, it springs from genuine curiosity. Her questions are deeply personal. "What if I wasn't so much a bad fisherman as a person struggling hopelessly against an ancient tribal destiny?" Sandor must have pondered this question for quite a while before writing it down; certainly did some research, as she later shares. The fact that the question is, in part, unanswerable lends it authenticity.

     Return to a scene or story that you've written. What question was driving your exploration? Write it out. Rewrite the piece incorporating your question.

Sandor's first three paragraphs contain multiple questions, but they all point in the same direction—toward a reconciliation of her fishing obsession with her Jewish heritage. Often when beginning writers discover that unanswerable questions are permissible, they err on the side of abundance. Too many questions diffuse a story's focus and diminish the influence of a good question. Questions can also heighten the reader's anxiety, as he or she searches for a single direction for the story's movement. Usually it is quite easy to reframe inessential questions as musing, declarative statements. Instead of asking, "Is there a prohibition against fishing on the Sabbath?" Sandor writes, "I wondered idly if there was a prohibition. . . ." A sentence that ends with a question mark rises above the rest, gaining the reader's attention.

Sandor's piece is also an illustration of another good policy: If it's possible to show, show. It's common in spiritual memoir for writers to digress into theological, psychological, or spiritual monologues; we are curious about the ideas behind reality. Abstract explorations are not inherently bad; in fact, they are stimulating for some readers. But stories have more universal appeal. If you are inclined to digress into philosophy, be aware that this can be a means of avoiding the gut-and-bones of personal experience. Pace your reflections so that they appear intermittently, in the midst of the story. Limit them in scope and length to give the reader space to digest them. And push yourself by asking, Can I show these ideas rather than tell them? Often you can place your ponderings in a colorful, appealing context.

After her guilt-ridden morning of fishing, Sandor finds herself pursuing questions at the college library's Judaica collection. She asks the librarian, "Just offhand, do you have anything on Jews and fishing?"

The librarian raised his eyebrows as high as they would go, then sighed. "I can see you've never been in here before. Listen, sweetheart, a Jewish fisherman is going to be as hard to dig up as a Jewish athlete. I mean, sure, we all want to be Sandy Koufax."

The librarian fills a two-tiered cart with books of "warnings, blessings, fish fables, advice, recipes, amulets, and gravestone symbology—the whole megillah." Sandor proceeds to share her findings, some praising and others scorning fish and their catchers. Instead of acquiring an instructive tone, these paragraphs use humor and informal banter to keep the information lively and to maintain continuity with the rest of the story. Sandor is still searching, only now she's using books. In this manner, she conveys the results of her research not as objective telling but as a scene of discovery. Not only that—Sandor's research unearths one of her grandmother's sayings ("Eat, or be eaten"), thus tying the telling directly to her past. What might have been a dry, informational rant is instead a seamless narrative.

A few years ago I wrote a short piece about a mystical, half-sleeping, half-waking dream I'd had—a full-bodied, wide-open rush of wind that roared through the bottoms of my feet and out the top of my head. In writing I debated: Can natural laws be suspended momentarily? What would be the psychological consequences? My writing grew dull, and yet sorting through what I believed about mysticism was my primary reason for writing. Then I remembered a series of conversations I had with a physicist friend from church. I recreated our dialogues in writing, allowing him to personify my own skepticism just as he had in real life. The story showed what I otherwise would have told;

the scenes of conversation and our respective relationships to church worship did the work of the piece.

> ❧ *Find a stretch of reflective writing within your memoir. Ask yourself, "What memory or anecdote helped inform these thoughts?" Try to find the lived experience that undergirds the reflections. Write the scene, revealing what you previously told with story.*

SUMMARIES AS TRANSITIONS

There is a difference between the reflective voice writers use to ponder life's mysteries and a summary. Summaries rehash what has already been said, or they pull together a bunch of ideas into one, broad statement. Occasionally you need to use a summary to bridge one story or idea to the next. Here's an example from Martha Manning's *Chasing Grace*:

> Receiving the sacrament of penance was just the beginning of my education about guilt and sin. With each year it seemed that my potential as a major sinner was increasing. I found out that I was guilty of infractions that I didn't even know were sins. Gradually, I became aware that there were things I had been doing almost my whole life that were actually grave offenses. Most of these behaviors were in the category of "impurity," which I was to learn much later was the euphemism for any concept or word related to sex.

Note how Manning leaps through time in this paragraph and how she transitions from the topic of penance to sex. The summary serves a useful purpose. But in isolation, it's not very interesting reading. Summaries rely on abstractions (guilt, sin, grave offenses) and sweeping statements. They work best when serving a purpose that furthers the story.

PRAISE AND THE REFLECTIVE VOICE

One form of telling is entirely unique to spiritual memoir—that of directly addressing the sacred in the midst of the story. Segues into prayer are most common among Christian writers (Augustine, Teresa of Avila, and Thomas Merton are prime examples), although you also find them occasionally among Native American authors. At the opening of *Black Elk Speaks*, Black Elk offers the sacred pipe up to the Great Spirit before beginning his story: "Grandfather, Great Spirit, lean close to the earth that you may hear the voice I send. You towards where the sun goes down, behold me; Thunder Beings, behold me!" Clearly the reader is a secondary audience. The reader recedes into the background as the writing becomes communication between writer and divinity.

Such direct address is less common in contemporary memoir, although the intent of offering one's story to a sacred presence often lies just below the surface. When I first discovered this propensity for direct address in spiritual memoir, I found it freeing: I could share my prayers with the reader; I could name the mystery to whom I was really writing rather than cloaking it in story. In a way, writing your prayers is a manner of showing. You may be speaking to the Sacred, but covertly you are showing the reader what your relationship is like. When we read Teresa of Avila's introduction, "May [this account] be to His glory and praise; and may it lead my confessors to know me better, and so help me in my weakness that I may be able to render some part of the service that I owe to the Lord," we gain a strong sense of her devotion to and reliance on God. She *shows* her prayer by *telling* it to God.

Temper your reflective writing by asking, Does this serve my story's thrust? The spiritual search drives the memoir forward. Reflection, on the page as in life, is an integral dimension of the spiritual search. The reflective voice—with insight, humor, curiosity, and awe—becomes the glue that holds narrative fragments together. It reveals the present day personality who contains the stories and gives them unity and import.

Finding a Structure for Your Story

ONE OF THE GREATEST challenges in putting together a memoir is discovering what framework will best hold your story. Structure is almost impossible to teach because the form a piece of writing takes should arise naturally from its content. You have to listen carefully to the nature of your story and imaginatively mirror that nature with a form. For example, a friend of mine is writing a spiritual memoir about growing up as a pastor's kid; Bill's technique for surviving the unnatural, "holy" role expected of him in a small, Midwestern town was to project himself into a fantasy world where he was a New York City sophisticate and was expressive, animated, and willful. The challenge of his spiritual journey was to bring his two personas together into one that is more genuinely himself. His memoir alternates stories of real hardship with humorous pieces from his imagined urban life until near the end, when the two worlds converge into the true Bill.

Early ideas for structure. It's rare that an author knows what form the story will take until at least one draft is complete. Only then do you have a full picture of the story and its shape. However, some people are unable to generate material without at least a vague vision of its structure. One student of mine couldn't conceive of her prolific writing as a book until she got the idea to use her body as a structure. In the story she describes a part of her body, its scars, and the memories it holds, moving from head to toe, over the course of the book. If you have ideas for a structure early on, that's great. Structure helps organize your thoughts; it keeps you motivated. One caution, however: Early structural ideas usually undergo lots of revision. Work within the structure you envision, but keep your mind open to possibilities that may better serve your story.

Chronology. A general rule of storytelling is to not depart from chronological order unless you have a good reason. We experience time chronologically, and so we're easily confused by stories that leap wildly back and forth in time. It's a rare memoir that doesn't use chronology as its backbone.

Using a front story. Memory adds a challenging dynamic to chronology because, although time moves forward, the present is often filled with flashbacks of the past. Following a chronology does not necessitate telling about your life from start to finish. Sometimes it is helpful to have a front story, a firm foothold in chronology that propels your memoir forward. For instance, let's say attending your cousin's bar mitzvah is the front story. As the celebration progresses, you recall your own bar mitzvah and its radical impact on your life, digressing from the front story to the past. This technique draws a clear link between the memory and its relevance to you today. Once you and your reader are established in a particular time (at your cousin's bar mitzvah), it's much easier to follow memory's whimsical leaps. Just don't forget to return to the front story and reveal how the memory intersects with the narrative present.

Sandwiching stories. Another possibility for structure, particularly for shorter pieces, is to sandwich one memory within another. The resonance and tension that arise between disparate narratives can enrich both. Bernard Cooper uses this technique in his short memoir, "Burl's." He begins and ends with a scene in which, as a child, he witnessed two men in drag outside a diner. Sandwiched inside this scene he places three other memories from boyhood, all of which reveal gender to be more confusing than we might expect.

Outline or map the structures of your favorite memoirs. The best way to learn about various forms for memoir is to study others' writing. When you admire an author's structure, take time to decipher how it works. There are as many structures as there are stories. Expanding your repertoire is always advantageous.

Revision as Seeing Anew

Most beginning writers confront the prospect of an overhaul of a manuscript with rebellious fury. The word *revision* sounds like an English teacher's torture implement. It implies that the initial go-round was inadequate. A first draft can seem carved in stone. You sweat blood getting those words down; isn't that enough? Or the rush that carried you through a first draft felt like inspiration; isn't tinkering with the manuscript sacrilegious? The excitement of writing, most people presume, resides in the spontaneity of the first draft. Anything beyond that is drudgery.

And yet "the holy work of making literature is in revision," as Carol Bly so blithely puts it. How can this be? Language is more like clay than stone. While revision is difficult, there is no aspect of the writing process that isn't. A bad attitude toward revision is a form of "better the devil you know." Once revision grows familiar, it loses its horns. Completing a rough draft is like dumping all the puzzle pieces out of the box, turning them right side up, and sorting out the edge pieces. Finally you know what you've got to work with. Only then can you start creating.

"Re-vision" is seeing anew. When we revise, we shine a new quality of light on our subject. Reading authors we admire, we can be astonished by their wisdom, by the accuracy of their memories, by the story's delightful structure, and by the grandiloquence of the language. "What amazing, brilliant people!" we think (with its subtle corollary, "I could never write like that"). These authors may be brilliant, but if the truth be known, they can't "write like that" either. At least not on the first try. Writing that is thoughtful, fluent, and stirring only comes with revision. Here's Patricia Hampl's take on it:

> Is it possible to convey the enormous degree of blankness, confusion, hunch, and uncertainty lurking in the act of writing? When I am the reader, not the writer, I too fall into the lovely illusion that the words before me which read so inevitably, must also have been written exactly as they appear, rhythm and cadence, language and syntax, the powerful waves of the sentences laying themselves on the smooth beach of the page one after another faultlessly.
>
> But here I sit before a yellow legal pad, and the long page of the preceding two paragraphs is a jumble of crossed-out lines, false starts, confused order. A mess. The mess of my mind trying to find out what it wants to say. This is a writer's frantic, grabby mind, not the poised mind of a reader waiting to be edified or entertained.

The experience of reading is misleading. It belies the chaos of the writing process with a polish that, when at its finest, makes writing appear casual. What strikes us as smart or beautiful got that way through many layers of work. If you look closely at the choices Hampl makes in the preceding paragraphs, you see evidence of revision. She crafts a long, undulating sentence to describe the smooth reading process, while she depicts writing in fragments, repetition, and harsh-sounding words. Hampl's sentence structure, use of punctuation, and word choices all *show* what the content *tells*. This isn't easy to accomplish. We may not notice such decisions on a quick read, but we feel them viscerally nonetheless.

Reading is like looking through a telescope at the stars—radiance jumps lightyears in an instant to dazzle your eyes. Writing is building that telescope, stacking lens after lens inside a structure. Any single lens magnifies the stars, but only so much. When the lenses are all together, the stars appear piercing and close.

This is good news. Your writing can be profoundly wise and elegant too, when the hard work of revision is complete. To fully grasp the possibilities of revision, however, you may need to revise some notions about the nature of writing.

First, it's important to know that revision occurs quite effortlessly between our different attempts at writing. Each time we begin a new story, we build on what we've learned from writing the last. We make slight changes in our approach based on what worked and what didn't, what we enjoyed and where we got hung up. These changes may be small and they are often unconscious, but they're significant nevertheless. The conceptual leap we make between pieces results from integrating past writing experiences with the growth that has occurred naturally in our personal lives.

Second, even though we gain literary skills with practice and study, we remain beginners with each new piece. The only book I know how to write is the one I've written. I have no clue how to write the next one and must begin learning from scratch. Gustav Mahler found this to be true regarding his fourth symphony:

This one is quite fundamentally different from my other symphonies. But that *must be*; I could never repeat a state of mind—and as life drives on, so too I follow new tracks in every work. That is why at first it is always so hard for me to get down to work. All the skill that experience has brought one is of no avail. One has to begin to learn all over again for the new thing one sets out to make. So one remains everlastingly a beginner! It is and always will be a gift of God—one that, like every loving gift, one cannot deserve and cannot get by asking.

Each work has its own form, language, and lessons, which we can only discover with a beginner's mind. At no point in a writing career does a manuscript emerge flawlessly. Seasoned writers are as confounded by a new piece as you are.

Third, most of us have the expectation, with good reason, that the second draft will be better than the first. After all, the whole point of revision is to bring urgency and refinement to our initial satisfactory but lackluster prose. Here I invite you to recall what it's like to clean a closet. At first the shelves are messy and familiar. But as soon as you begin opening the Parcheesi box to count all the pieces and separating 1967's holiday cards from 1968's, the chaos of the closet spills into the room. The hour-long project balloons to fill the whole weekend. The closet, like revision, gets much worse before it gets better. We take memories out to examine them more closely; we sort and rearrange them, and try on organizational structures. It's perfectly natural for the writing to become more chaotic on its way to a new order.

Fourth, we have to remember that once our stories are on the page, they still have an energy, a will, and a voice all their own. Writing is like giving birth. That first draft is your baby; it needs attention, nourishing, and love. It comes from you, but it is quite separate from you. Sooner or later you realize it has a sharp independent streak and a quirky personality. Eventually your hopes for the child fall by the wayside as it discovers for itself who it wants to become.

Revision is essentially an act of listening. The first draft is flushed, active, and stunning, just like a newborn. But it needs to grow up. Your job is to listen for the piece's heartbeat—the core, what pumps life through every pore—and nurture that beat until it grows strong. Your story's heartbeat is rarely what you first expect it to be. This is especially deceptive with memoir, when you think you know the subject like the back of your hand.

To understand what I mean by a story's heartbeat, it helps to distinguish between the overt subject and the covert subject. The overt subject is what's obvious—your mother's death, your pilgrimage to Lhasa, your years in a cult. The overt subject is what you tell yourself you are writing from the start. When I first began writing my memoir, *Swinging on the Garden Gate*, I told myself I was writing about my bike trip in Wales. After I finished writing the story, I read it and discovered it was really a spiritual journey; what most intrigued me were the changes that happened in my relationship to the sacred. So I went back and rewrote it with that lens, adding stories from before and after to give the bike trip context. Once these other memories fell into place, I recognized how my relationship with the sacred had been affected by my sexuality and sexual identity. A grand theme in my life has been discovering how my body informs me about the sacred. Reconciling sexuality and spirituality was my covert subject, the memoir's heartbeat. This covert subject felt right, and ripe. I went back to the drawing table and rewrote the whole thing.

Writing is a means of engaging mystery. In the first draft, the unknown we face is, What am I going to write? How might this subject emerge? The flurry of surprises that follow are the fruits of reaching into that unknown. Engagement with mystery doesn't end with the completion of a rough draft; rather, its nature changes. During revision the unknown is, What gives this subject life? This more fertile mystery is the story's covert subject. We must find the story's interior life and reconcile it with its outer appearance. At first this happens at the story's gut level, as we discover what it is really about. Later we can help the covert subject move outward through the structure and craft of language.

At one point in my life I was curious about prayer: Why do I bother? I wrote to find out. I began by describing the sensation of bending to my knees—an old fashioned custom I maintain. As I wrote, I was reminded of a time when I was ten years old and sleeping in my grandmother's bed. My grandparents had twin beds, and when I visited after my grandfather's death, my grandmother took the taller of the two, giving me her own. My grandmother came in late at night, waking me up. Silently I watched her undress and slip into her nightgown. Then, without knowing I was watching, she fell to her knees before my grandfather's empty bed.

Since I know to trust my mind's bizarre leaps, I wrote this story as well as the story of my grandfather's death. When I arrived at the end of my first draft, I faced a puzzle: What exactly did Gramps' death have to do with my morning prayer? I returned to the beginning to find out.

By holding these two stories together, trusting that they had something to reveal to me, I eventually discovered that deep prayer is like a death experience for me—something I both long for and fear. It took many drafts for me to discover an answer to my initial question, and many more drafts to craft my story so that it was seamless. When the piece was complete, I had a new knowledge of what happens within me during prayer.

In essence revision isn't about reshaping manuscript pages; it's about reshaping your self. As you write out memories, the discoveries you make change you and change your perspective on those memories. Then you can return to the beginning again, allowing your new clarity to shine through the manuscript from the start. Resistance to revision may really be resistance to growth. Revising can be wrenching and a truckload of work, but the transformation wrought on you and your manuscript is well worth your while.

How, then, do we discover the covert subjects lurking at the periphery of our awareness? The first order of business is for the writing ego to step aside; we must be open to the likelihood that we don't know what our story is about. We have to believe that our story has as much to say as we do. That baby has its own talents, short-comings, and dreams—a life and will all its own. Once we trust this, we are able to listen for what the story wants. So the challenge of revision is this: How can we get enough distance from the subject to see it in a new light? How can we step away from our agenda so we can hear the story's still, small voice?

The Back Burner

The best way to distance yourself from your subject so that you can see it in a new light is to give yourself time. Brenda Ueland, author of *If You Want to Write*, went on five-mile walks, allowing her brain to cavort freely and giving her perspective on her work. A poet friend of mine purposefully abstains from reading her drafts for a week. The first time I got feedback from a mentor on my memoir, her comments so infuriated me I swore I'd never speak to her again nor write another word. Three months later I dug the manuscript out of the recycling and discovered, much to my chagrin, that my mentor's comments were smart. I also discovered that my writing was not half-bad. If you are engrossed in your subject, you are working on it whether or not your pen hits the paper. Ideas whirl in the back of your brain; memories mutate and shift. These unconscious, effortless mechanisms perform wonders. You look away from the subject only to see it more closely.

Time is a good test of your subject's viability. If after a month's hiatus you've become uninterested in writing about Aunt Jenny's breviary, that's an important sign. The subjects that are the crux of your existence—your life-long questions, your soul's themes—only intensify with age. If this doesn't happen, throw Aunt Jenny's breviary out the window. Either that or ask yourself why you thought it was significant in the first place. Search beneath the obvious for the undercurrent of passion. When your topics skim the surface rather than probe for heart and meaning, they tend to go stale.

Carol Bly calls revision the "long middle stage" of writing, when we allow our memories and ideas to simmer. It's the stage most beginning writers skip. Sometimes life itself provides the interruptions and consequent transformations that allow us to add another insightful layer to a manuscript. More often we don't have (or don't choose) the luxury of growing into our subject, and instead relentlessly plow forward for good or ill. In this case, using methods other than simply waiting can give us the fresh perspective we need.

A Writer's Journal

The writer's journal is a powerful tool. Whether it is a notebook or computer file doesn't matter, as long as it is outside your manuscript and you can rant, experiment, ask questions, use your natural voice, and generally explore a subject with as much freedom as you need. Virginia Woolf recorded the emotional swings of her writing process in her diaries and was then able to recognize patterns in her panic and elation. By keeping a writer's journal, I learned that the period after I finish a piece is a dangerous time. I turn melancholic and avoid grief by leaping prematurely into a new project. The journal provides distance for me to learn that, if I'm patient with the fallow months, my creative well will be restored. The emotional remove and privacy of a journal are invaluable to the revision process.

I keep both a computer file journal and a paper notebook. When the ideas are flying, I like the speed of the keyboard; I also like its capacity to cut and paste. But a fountain pen and college-ruled notebook are comforting, especially when I'm insecure about what's happening in my writing. Writing by hand slows me down; it accesses a quieter part of my brain and sometimes provides insights I'd never get at the computer. The notebook also allows me to sketch out the shape of my piece with greater ease.

At the beginning of a revision, use your journal to ask yourself, What is really going on here? It's not an unfamiliar question; hopefully you've been asking it all along. But now that you've finished a draft, your answer may have changed. Another way to ask this question is, Why am I writing this? What's in it for me? This may seem like an egotistical question, but it's terrifically important. Whatever is at stake for the narrator becomes the reader's investment. Your story's emotional edge (what nags at you) should grow ever sharper.

Another essential way to use your journal is to ask, What more do I have to say about this subject? Often revision simply means generating more material. Invariably you know, feel, and believe more about the subject than is evidenced in the first draft. The journal allows you to digress, reminisce, free associate, and unabashedly ramble without having to worry about what the reader thinks. This looseness of mind uncovers layers of emotion and links between disparate thoughts; it enables a certain playfulness in prose that the carved-in-stone strictures of the first draft never permit.

Read the Draft for Clues

The first draft drops big clues about the story's heartbeat. For this reason, it's important to save copies of your drafts, either on paper or in the computer. When you revise, work on a copy of the original. This preserves the helpful clues that reside in the original. It also allows you to return to the first draft's spontaneous voice should you dislike your revision, thus freeing you from the fear of your story growing worse.

An English professor at my college had a reputation for giving harsh criticism to student papers. There was even a rumor that he cut one paper to shreds and handed it back to the student in a plastic baggie. But he gave this advice in a lecture once, and it's stuck with me ever since: When you're writing a thesis, state your hypothesis in your opening paragraph. Write the body of your essay exploring that hypothesis. End with a conclusion that draws together your thinking on the subject. Then, he said, take a pair of scissors and cut your conclusion off the bottom. Move it to the top of a new page, and start all over.

I still groan at the thought. But this ruthless professor knew that we don't have a clue what we think about a subject until we have written it out. Only at the end do we get a glimpse of our true insights. While his advice doesn't directly apply to memoir (God forbid we write summative paragraphs at the end of our stories!), the concept is invaluable. Often the end of the first draft has wandered away from the overt subject and touches something surprising and valuable. What does the end of your draft know that the beginning does not? Take this information back to the beginning and allow it to inform your revision.

Another thing to watch for in your first draft is an image or metaphor that holds particular power for you. Often these images are the places where you've done your best writing; sometimes they appear in scenes you've referred back to elsewhere in the manuscript. The senses in those passages are acute and the emotion fierce. These are usually the images that raise strong feelings, positive or negative, that you don't completely understand. As a result, these images point to what really matters in the story.

In a way, listening to your first draft is like listening to a dream. You must "dream the dream onward," as Carl Jung advised, by allowing your memoir's images to become fully realized. Try taking an image from your first draft—say, your favorite pair of overalls—and dialoguing with it in your writer's journal, allowing it to speak in its own voice. "What are you trying to say to me?" you might ask the overalls. They reply, "You wear me when you're most relaxed. How come that's so rarely?" Or reminisce in your journal, exploring all the memories and ideas the image conjures up. (The first pair of overalls I ever owned I bought at a garage sale in southern Minnesota; I love babies in overalls; my sister thought a ghost lived in her overall bib pocket when she was little—she called it the Boo.) Exploring the cultural associations with an image to discover how others might see it can also be illuminating. (Overalls are farmer's work clothing; they are the ultimate informal wear; isn't it a stereotype that lesbians wear overalls?) Give the image many opportunities to speak and to steer you toward the heart of your story.

If an image in your rough draft has emotional potency for you, it is trustworthy. It doesn't matter whether that image came from your memory, a dream, your imagination, a painting, or *People* magazine; its truth resides in the emotional link it has to your gut. Half of the hard work of becoming a writer is learning to trust your intuition, which entails believing that the images with resonance for you have actual import. A good (and necessary) revision exercise is to linger on your central images, expanding their scenes with details and weaving in any reflections you gain.

Listening to your rough draft may be as simple as noting where the writing shines. Often we hit our stride writing those scenes that hold special intrigue. If there are sentences or whole sections that seem unusually cohesive, circle them. What do they teach about the story's energy? Dialogue with these scenes or reenter them, writing loosely to allow them to take you in a new direction. Don't let the fine prose inhibit you from playing or from striving to refine it further. Beautiful writing in a first draft is a rare thing; it is a brass key with potential to unlock further treasures. For this reason, it is always worth paying attention to your own surprising brilliance.

As soon as you think you've got a grasp of your covert subject, write it on an index card as a single, simple sentence. This is not easy.

But it's good practice for all the times you have to explain what you're writing about to inquisitive friends, and comes in handy when you write inquiry letters to publishers. A single-sentence description forces you to focus your energy in a specific direction. As you work your way through the second draft, return again and again to that note. Ask yourself how each scene fulfills this intention. You may rewrite your sentence four or five times before your project is complete, as your focus becomes clearer. Even though your statement is not set in stone, it will help you move forward and unify the overt and covert subjects of your story.

A similar exercise is to create working titles along the way. While not as directive as a concise statement of purpose, a working title can still steer you. Besides, titles often need as much revision as the writing does. Rarely does a writer find a successful title on the first go-round. You may as well start searching early.

Mapping the Story

Another way to gain distance from your manuscript is to represent your story's movement visually. Try drawing a map of your rough draft. This gives you a bird's-eye view of your material and, therefore, the distance you need to figure out what to do next. The map can take the form of an outline or a drawing. Outlines can be obstacles for first drafts, as the structures they provide inevitably prove faulty and can actually hinder creative digression and free association. But during the revision stages, call up all of your fifth-grade teacher's lessons in Roman numerals. What happens in each paragraph? What are the overt and covert subjects? This process may seem awkward at first since memoirs are largely narrative and rarely have topic sentences. But every story has a reflective underbelly, a building of emotional awareness or conceptual understanding that happens beneath the action. An outline helps you see what's really going on.

If you sketch a visual map of a draft ask yourself, What is its dramatic shape? A mountain? A spiral? A crescendo followed by a decrescendo? As best as possible, represent the energetic movement of your writing with a visual image. This exercise is a way of listening to your story's natural form. Whatever shape you discover in the drawing, you can then keep it in your awareness during revision. Revision is call-and-response—the writer listens, learns, and puts the learning into action. When you're stringing together multiple scenes, your map may look like stepping stones across a stream. Then it's helpful to ask, How do I get from scene A to scene B? The map challenges you to find the conceptual bridges between anecdotes, the themes that unify your narrative. With a map it is easy to move huge chunks of story around and visually grasp the impact. What if you moved the climactic scene to the beginning? What would happen if you cut out these memories? Since you're playing in your notebook and not with your actual memoir, there's nothing to lose by experimenting.

At the literary center where I teach there are writing studios for rent. One whole wall of each studio is covered with a bulletin board. If the memoir you're working on isn't terrifically long, it's a fun exercise to cut your first draft into chunks and pin them up on the wall. Try reorganizing them in a variety of ways—by theme, by chronology, by liturgical or natural seasons, by increasing tension. With the pages on a board, you can literally step back from your story and work with structure in a flexible, visual way.

How Much Detail?

When we return to our initial drafts to expand scenes, the question, How much detail is enough? often arises. We've all read description that bores us to tears—every blasted nick and dent on that Chevy truck the author obviously adores and about which we don't give a rip. Where is the threshold between using enough details to fully evoke a scene and so many that we lose the reader's interest?

To a degree, the amount of detail you include is a matter of style. Some writers prefer a slow pace, milking each image before continuing. Contemporary readers (and writers) have a tendency to like fast-paced stories and have a low tolerance for elaborate descriptions. Neither choice is more literary or successful, although it might influence your publishing possibilities. In either case, it's essential to include only those details that do the work of your piece. The description, however short or long, must shed light on the story's heart. Does the description ground the reader in place and body? Does it allow the reader to see, feel, smell, or hear what's important in a way that's unique and striking? If you're writing about a shamanic drum journey and your story's heart is the link between yourself and the pulse of the earth, you can sustain description of the drum's resonant sound, its reverberation off the walls and in your bones, and how your own heartbeat joined the shaman's rhythm for quite a while without losing your reader's interest. If, however, your story's heart is your connection with the animal totem that appeared in a vision during the drum journey, the sound of the drum doesn't do much work in the story. You may mention it, particularly if it induces the altered state that allows the totem to appear, but it's best not to linger on a detail that doesn't point toward what's at stake. In general, allow details space in proportion to the work that they accomplish. If they do a lot of work, linger with the description. If they are extraneous or distracting, cut them.

Here are a few other miscellaneous revision exercises that can give you the distance necessary to see your subject anew.

Double the length of your manuscript. If your memoir is four pages, make it eight. Don't add any more content—that is, don't tack on another scene—but rather go into more detail and reflective depth with the content that's already there. This exercise forces you to expand your memory and therefore listen to it closely.

Halve the length of your manuscript. If your first draft is four pages, rewrite it to be two. Only do this exercise if you've tried the doubling exercise first. Both overwriters and underwriters can benefit from the doubling and halving exercises. It's important to flesh the story out first and discover what's really going on. Only then is it worthwhile to condense your discoveries into a concise, tight story. Halving forces you to do away with the extraneous; you must choose those images, scenes, and reflections that work for you—and toss the rest.

Rewrite your manuscript without looking at the earlier draft. I'm serious—don't peek. The point is not to replicate the first draft but to open yourself to a new version of the story as told from this moment rather than that of your initial writing. If new details or digressions emerge, go with them. Don't be distracted if your writing seems poorer than the first draft; you can always go back and fold your new insights into earlier writing.

Intentionally write digressions. Our biggest insights often come when we let our minds drift away from our subject, to another memory or anecdote, and follow its lead. If we keep our thoughts on a tight leash while we write, we miss out on the whimsical meanderings that lead to real intimacy with our subject. Of course, digression may be a form of avoidance or a pleasant distraction. Still, those digressions that strike gold are worth many stabs in the dark. Some helpful questions are: If I were to digress wildly in this scene, what would I write? When else did I feel this way? What other memories are relevant here? When deciding which digressions to keep, take Phillip Lopate's advice: "The digression must wander off the point only to fulfill it."

Imagine telling your story to someone in an elevator. In the time it takes to travel twenty stories, how would you tell the plot of your memoir? Pay attention to the natural order of your telling, as it may help you to structure your writing. What details or episodes do you instinctually skip? Which do you elaborate? Allow these prominence in your manuscript.

Read your draft aloud. My cat always leaves the room at this stage. I'm a stickler for reading aloud because language is meant to be heard. Reading your draft aloud alerts you to its rhythm and cadence in a way that silent readings never do. Reading aloud (or better yet, recruiting a loved one to read your words back to you) is especially useful toward the end of the writing process as you begin to attend to word choice, sentence structure, and the more cosmetic attributes of craft. Reading aloud distances you from the story's content and highlights its sound.

FEEDBACK

Perhaps the most effective way to gain perspective on your writing is to see it through another's eyes. Receiving feedback requires a dose of courage and a thickening of the skin, but in the long run it is an invaluable skill. How a reader experiences your story can radically change your understanding of it.

Just because you trust someone with your life doesn't mean you can trust him or her with your writing. The quality of feedback you obtain has little to do with how much the reader loves you. In fact, family and friends are often the worst people to share your writing with while it is in middraft. They are too caught up in their relationship with you to view your writing as a work-in-progress quite separate from yourself. Good feedback is hard to find. Work with a writing buddy, a serious reader, or a teacher who can articulate why he or she is engaged (or not) in your story.

Once you've found a trustworthy reader (or even better, a writers' group), keep in mind that every reader's experience is different and therefore relative. Readers' responses are frequently contradictory. You have the ultimate say-so with your manuscript, even if there's consensus around a criticism. But remember that the point of getting feedback is to "see your work anew." There's nothing better than a fresh pair of eyes to do that for you. If you disagree with feedback, be clear with yourself as to why. Is it because the reader doesn't understand your purpose? Then perhaps you need to clarify your purpose. Is it because you want to avoid a painful memory or a difficult subject? Then perhaps your disagreement is getting in the way of deepening the manuscript. Every response a reader gives you is true to his or her experience of your story. If that person's experience isn't what you want it to be, revise the manuscript.

Be straightforward with your readers about the type of feedback you are looking for. Don't allow them to bog you down with feedback about the story's cosmetics when you still don't hear its heartbeat.

Early on in the revision process, when you're searching for your story's center of gravity, it's helpful to ask readers, "What's this really about for you?" Others can often see a story's covert agenda more clearly than you can. It's also good to ask, "What intrigues you? Confuses you? Where do you want more? Where do you want less?" Ask middraft readers to identify the most powerful scene or the place where your writing shines, as these may point to the story's heartbeat. Later on you can ask for help with finding an effective structure, bridging transitions, and finally, tightening your sentences and other cosmetic touch-ups. Be clear about the kind of feedback you're looking for before readers begin reading, as this will influence how they read and perhaps save everyone time.

Getting feedback is about gathering information, not putting your writing on trial. There's no need to be defensive about what you've written or to explain what you really mean. Simply jot down your readers' comments for later reflection. When they ask questions as part of their feedback, write the questions down before you answer them aloud. Questions that arise in a reader's mind need to be answered in the writing, not in conversation. Some teachers prohibit writers from speaking during feedback time for this very reason. Take notes when you receive feedback so that you don't get caught up in a conversation about the writing and forget the readers' reactions.

Quality feedback is invaluable, but it's possible to get too much of it too early in the revision process. Remember that revision is primarily about listening for what the story wants. After the story feels satisfied and whole, you can attend to your own needs and the needs of your audience.

The Audience

Midway through revision it is helpful to think directly about the audience. Prior to this, you have spent the majority of your energy getting the story out, searching for what it is really about, and helping it grow; thoughts for the audience have taken a backseat to the demands of the story itself and to your own needs. But now it is constructive to imagine an audience (be they loved ones or the mass market) journeying through your pages.

Memoir is like a house you've inhabited for a long time. The readers are long-anticipated guests. What can you do to make your guests feel welcome? You must ease their entrance, pique their interest, and entice them to stay with treats and engaging dialogue. Using a conversational (and not a didactic or formal) voice helps your guests be at ease. Beware of inside jokes or references that may feel alienating. Arrange the furniture so that your guests don't trip over it during their tour. Don't rush your guests, but don't bore them with miscellany. A thorough dusting and sweeping prior to arrival is not only polite; it makes your lamps shine brighter and floorboards sparkle. By the time you usher your guests out the door, be sure that their stomachs are full, their minds captivated, and their hearts wider for having visited.

In other words, be a gracious host within the realm of your story. During the final stages of revision, the reader's needs can guide you in making your memoir accessible and giving it broad appeal. It is helpful —essential even—to get feedback at this stage. Any places where readers stumble need your attention. If they keep pointing out the elephant in the living room, perhaps you ought to mention the elephant. Transitions from one scene or time frame to the next need to be bridged gracefully. Connections between disparate themes need to be drawn. Word choices must be carefully examined and sentences tightened so that the surface experience of the language is animated. Even if you have no intention of sharing your end product with a broader audience, these final revisions are worthwhile as they continue to yield surprises and revelations.

All of this work can be delightful if approached like a puzzle. In final drafts, our work is to craft language so it both shows and tells, so the sense and sound of the words are matched as closely as possible. This careful tweaking can be very satisfying as all the final pieces slip into place. After all, you're preparing to welcome others into the intimacies of your memories and spiritual life. It's worth doing with care and panache.

FINAL TOUCHES

The following checklist of cosmetic changes will help you clean up your manuscript's surface and make your writing sparkle. If you enjoy playing with words, it's easy to be drawn into this type of revision work too early. Remember to make all your large structural and thematic changes first. Otherwise, you may spend precious time fiddling with word choices for a scene that you will later cut.

Paragraph length. Varying the length of your paragraphs helps sustain the reader's interest. Don't be afraid of short paragraphs; they can effectively emphasize a part of your story by setting it apart. Including too many short paragraphs, however, dilutes all your points. Don't be afraid of long paragraphs either, particularly when you're expanding a scene. But too many long paragraphs grow laborious. Check your manuscript for diversity.

Sentence structure. Simple, complex, short, long, lists, appositive clauses, dependent clauses, fragments, run-ons, dashes, semicolons, colons . . . the more you vary the structure of your sentences, the more you'll keep readers on their toes. Remember to retain your natural voice throughout. When you speak, you use a wide range of sentences. It's this diversity—and not a stiff, English-major style—that you want to represent on the page. Keep in mind that sentences that break rules (fragments, run-ons) pack the most punch when used sparingly. Beware of prepositional strings that dilute sentences ("I had a sense of a feeling of repulsion"); tightening them to be as concise as possible ("I was repulsed").

Show with paragraph and sentence structure. Sometimes it's possible to demonstrate the content of paragraphs and sentences with their structure. For example, here's Zora Neale Hurston describing a jazz performance:

> This orchestra grows rambunctious, rears on its hind legs and attacks the tonal veil with primitive fury, rending it, clawing it until it breaks through to the jungle beyond. I follow those heathen—follow them exultingly. I dance wildly inside myself; I yell within, I whoop; I shake my assegai above my head, I hurl it true to the mark yeeeooww! I am in the jungle and living the jungle way. My face is painted red and yellow, and my body is painted blue. My pulse is throbbing like a war drum. I want to slaughter something—give pain, give death to what, I do not know. But the piece ends. The men of the orchestra wipe their lips and rest their fingers. I creep back slowly to the veneer we call civilization with the last tone and find the white friend sitting motionless in his seat, smoking calmly.

"Good music they have here," he remarks, drumming the
table with his fingertips.

Note how Hurston's sentences pulse and even disintegrate with exuberance. Her simple sentence, "But the piece ends," mirrors the performance's abrupt closure. Her friend's blank comment (which is given its own short paragraph) and the flat way she describes it (as a remark rather than a compliment or praise) contrast sharply with her own experience, depicted in a lengthy, colorful paragraph. When a sentence or paragraph can illustrate its meaning with its form—when it both shows and tells—the congruity produces a stunning read. Choose only specific, climactic, sensory passages for this type of intense rewrite. Careful construction like this can be difficult to sustain at first. The more you practice crafting sentences, however, and observe examples in others' prose, the more it grows instinctual.

Dialogue. In scenes where significant action occurs, be sure to change summarized conversations into dialogue. You may not precisely remember what was said, but it's nonetheless worth the effort to recreate the conversation as best you can. Dialogue helps scenes come alive; it allows the reader to participate more fully in your memory. Likewise, consider whether the summarized conversations you don't deem significant enough to separate into dialogue may be effectively eliminated.

Word choice. Think about your words. Do they say exactly what you mean? Or is there a more precise choice? Scan your manuscript for all its hot-button words—the words you lean on to make meaning, the words you borrow from religious tradition, and the more general terms where you draw conclusions—and examine them closely. Often the refinement of a few words makes a tremendous difference in communicating intent. Also check for repeated use of the same word, adding variety where you can. This is the stage that wears out your thesaurus. Avoid the high school student's temptation to find flowery words to impress the reader. Instead, look for words that are exact and natural.

Active verbs. Check your manuscript for passive constructions (sentences without an active subject). These are particularly common when writers feel they need to hide the "I" for fear of egotism. They write, "The prayers were forgotten" rather than the more direct "I forgot the prayers." Active verbs strengthen your voice. Of all the words to fuss over, verbs pack the most punch. If you replace an ordinary verb with an unexpected one, your sentence jolts off the page. Note Hurston's verbs describing the orchestra—it "rears on its hind legs and attacks the tonal veil with primitive fury, rending it, clawing it." The animalistic verbs she chooses help us hear the music as she does.

General versus specific nouns. An easy way to make your prose dazzle is to change generalizations to specifics. Instead of gazing out your window at a tree, let your reader know it's a mountain ash. If you're describing how your mind wanders during meditation, mention the grocery list and dirty cat litter that float through your brain. Wherever possible, give specific examples to illustrate your story.

Clichéd language. Scan your manuscript for well-worn phrases and rewrite them with more accurate and unique language. "I was going crazy," "The day flew by," "My heart leapt," and other such expressions are fine in normal conversation, but on the page they are overly familiar. If you can articulate your experience more specifically, both the writing and the reading will be more stimulating. *How* did you feel crazy? How else can you depict the swift passage of time? If your heart didn't literally leap, what *did* happen? Clichés signal laziness. Revising them forces you to name your experiences.

The royal we. It's natural to slip into the "we" voice, particularly during reflective writing. However, "we" is an increasingly hazardous point of view, given our multicultural society and growing global awareness. Be certain that your "we" includes all of humanity and not just your subgroup (middle-class white Americans, for instance, or Roman Catholics), and specify whom you mean when your "we" is a subgroup. Rewrite passages that expound using the royal "we" with the more intimate "I," and note the difference. Then your choice to use the "we" voice will be deliberate. Take heed of Thoreau's words in the introduction to *Walden*: "In most books the I, or first person, is omitted; in this it will be retained; that, in respect to egotism, is the main difference. We commonly do not remember that it is, after all, always the first person that is speaking."

Title. Titles are challenging. Your title must grab the reader and point to the heart of your story. Give it careful thought. What does your title reveal about you, the narrator? Does it evoke the central mystery or tension of your story without giving too much away? Does it hint at both covert and overt subjects?

Ending. "Stories have to end," Dennis Covington wrote in *Salvation on Sand Mountain*. "Endings . . . grow inevitably from the stories themselves. The ending of a story only seems inevitable, though, after it's over and you're looking back." When an ending is right, it feels balanced with the beginning, it grounds the reader in a new place or thought toward which the story has been pointing, and it leaves the reader with something to chew on. Summaries rarely work well for endings, whereas a scene can be surprisingly successful.

Endings needn't answer a question or solve a problem, but they should arrive at a different place from where the story began. An ending is a measure of movement—how much the writer (and therefore the reader) has grown in relation to the subject. This doesn't mean you should introduce a new subject in the final paragraphs, but rather add an unexpected twist to an old subject. Endings need to package the story so readers carry it with them after they close the book.

Beginning. Frequently a book's opening is the last thing an author writes. Those first sentences and paragraphs are crucial—potential readers will decide whether or not to commit to your story depending on the opening. You must introduce yourself, what is at stake, and the manner in which your story will be told, all in a short space. Like the title, the opening must elicit your story's heart without giving too much away. Often the end of a story teaches us how to begin it. Consider starting with an image or scene that contains the essence of the entirety. Always begin where the action begins. Explanatory background paragraphs rarely work well up front. You can always flash back later to fill readers in once you've gotten their attention.

When to Stop Revising

My mother always worries that I'll fall down revision's black hole and never return. It's a valid concern; I'm a certified perfectionist. For many beginning writers, the fear that they won't know when to stop revising inhibits them from revising at all. When it comes to working with memories, the well of insights is limitless, so it's possible to rewrite a memoir over a lifetime, adding layer upon layer of understanding, and never be finished. Memoirs may take years to write, but in the end they are like snapshots. They capture an instant that then passes; the lens's angle and the momentary perceptions of the eye peering through it are irretrievable. If you rework old material past its relevance, you will get stuck in that material and inhibit your personal growth. Bringing a piece to completion requires compassion for the incomplete self that is represented in the manuscript. Your true self continues to grow and change beyond the bounds of the printed story, but this does not make that portrait, now frozen in time, any less true. When my memoir hit the bookstores, two years had passed since my final revision. My theology had changed radically, and my interest in sexuality and spirituality had waned. It required great care for my former self (and for the readers who identified with her) to give the book marketing attention. Now when I read those pages it's from a distance, like seeing a photograph of my twenty-eight-year-old self. I disagree with her, I'm embarrassed by some of her ideas, but I'm generally proud she did such a marvelous job of sharing her truth.

In the course of working with new writers, I've become convinced that completion is possible and recognizable for most projects. When a piece is done, it feels plump and sound; the beginning and end balance like seats of the see-saw; the narrator's voice is consistent throughout; transitions ease the reader from one moment to the next; the important scenes are fleshed out; and the reader has a sense of movement from start to close. Questions aren't necessarily answered, and mysteries aren't necessarily solved, but there is movement. The narrator and reader inhabit a new understanding by the end. A complete manuscript is a lot like a gangly eighteen-year-old heading off to college or a job. It's full-grown, with an established personality and resolve, but it hasn't yet withstood the trials of independence. Only by venturing into the world, without the writer's parental oversight, will your memoir achieve a life of its own.

All this is to say we need to listen intently to our memories with a consideration that is not possible in a single draft. If memories are sacred stories and our means for discerning holiness in the world, then revision is a form of meditation or prayer. The sacred movements our memoirs reveal gain their life through contemplation.

Lest you think revision sounds like an awful lot of wasted time, consider the mighty iceberg: It takes a huge body below the surface to support the icy tip. The words you see in any published work are that shining tip; there is a proportional mass of writing you cannot see supporting the final product. This is true of any art—the thick layers below the painting's surface, the hours of movement behind the dancer's performance. How similar this is to the spiritual life, where strata of experience and thought and prayer undergird each glimmer of clarity. Texture and depth come to writing only with reworking. While the reader will never see the cut paragraphs, faulty digressions, and pages of journal writing, he or she will feel their gravity behind the words that do make it to print.

Learning to Read as a Writer

THERE ARE ONLY TWO tried-and-true tasks required to learn to write well: Write lots and read lots. Throughout this book I've used examples from the writers who have been my greatest teachers. Any writer you admire can become a personal writing instructor once you are engaged in the writing process and know how to read as a writer. The following hints will help you continue to learn about spiritual memoir beyond the bounds of this book. A resource list appears at the conclusion to get you started.

Always read for pleasure first. When you read as a writer, you're out to discover how an author creates responses, positive or negative, within the reader. But if you jump into this analytical mindset too soon, it's possible to lose sight of your immediate, visceral reaction to the story. Allow yourself to read naturally, fast or slow, obsessively or leisurely. When you feel delight, boredom, anxiety, suspense, or any other reaction, be aware of the sensation and keep reading. Your only jobs when reading for pleasure are to read naturally and to develop awareness about your natural responses.

Reread the books you admire. Once you've received a book's gifts, then you can return to it to ask, How did the author make me feel this way? How did he give me this insight? How did she make that scene so graphic or create such a unique structure? Reread books looking for the choices the author made when crafting the story. Some of the author's brilliance may be sheer luck, but most of literature's shine is hard-earned skill and lots of revision. It's instructive to assume that everything in a book is the result of the author's deliberate choices.

Mark up the book. If writing in books is a mortal sin to you, make photocopies of your favorite passages so you can highlight, star, and underline freely. What transitions strike you as smart? What details, word choices, or sentence structures stand out? Where do you observe foreshadowing? When does the author use a narrative voice and when a reflective voice? How does the author transition between them? Look closely at the beginning and ending of books, as these are often the hardest parts to write. How does the author unmask his or her persona? Introduce the subject? Bring about the sensation of closure? Make prolific notes in the margins.

Write journal entries in response to your reading. High school English teachers teach something we sometimes forget as adults: If you write about what you read, you not only understand the reading better, your awareness of your response is more precise. Writing your reactions to influential books helps you participate more thoroughly in the author's story. It also helps seal the story in memory—a great boon for those of us who forget books quickly.

Read your favorite passages aloud. Well-crafted writing is meant to be heard. What does it feel like to have another's pace and cadence roll off your tongue? Listen for sentence length, rhythm, repeated sounds, and innovative word choices. Can you gain a sense of the emotional content simply from its sounds?

Copy out your favorite passages. Holding another writer's exact sentence structure, rhythm, and sound in your body and allowing it to emerge from your pen can widen your repertoire. It may seem inane, as if you're a monk back in medieval Europe, but the slow practice of copying passages by hand helps you grow attentive to language. This exercise has the added benefit of sharpening your memory of what you've read.

Imitate your favorite passages or styles. Imitation is an old fashioned but invaluable exercise. When you find yourself saying, "I wish I could write like that!" pretend you can. Imagine yourself as Virginia Woolf , V. S. Naipal, or James Baldwin; take on that role model's voice and use it in your own material. This exercise is time consuming but extraordinarily useful. It forces you to step out of your worn writing patterns and try on an entirely new style. You might write your first successful run-on sentence. You might use vocabulary that otherwise isn't available to you. You might make a grandiose, philosophical statement for the first time. Imitative writing stretches your writing capacity. It's important to go back to your own, unique voice (which is infinitely better than any borrowed voice), but you'll return with new skills under your belt.

Putting It Out There

DURING THE FINAL STAGES of revision, it's time to face head-on the question of what to do with your manuscript. Tuck it under the bed? Make it into paper airplanes? Photocopy it and distribute it to your in-laws? Self publish? Pull out excerpts to send to magazines? Or confront the ruthless realm of agents and publishing? Once the writing process is complete, you have an end product—a story—with life and breath all its own. Your baby is now a young adult who is able to shake new employers' hands with confidence and converse with strangers without your hovering guidance. Letting your story go is no easier than dealing with an empty nest. The writing process may be complete, but the spiritual journey of working with memoir continues, thrusting your story into the world.

When I worked in retreat ministry, we used to draw the infinity sign to illustrate a pattern in spiritual growth. When you lead a healthy spiritual life, the journey inward, represented by one loop, counterbalances the journey outward, represented by the second loop. The journey inward is silence, prayer, reflection, receptivity—what happens when we withdraw from society to attend to the still, small voice within. The journey outward is service, relationship, and community—our interaction with others and the environment. In reality the two journeys blur, but the image of the infinity sign's balancing of internal and external work can help keep unhealthy tendencies in check. If teaching and volunteer work cram my every moment, I know it's time to step back. If meditation dominates my day to the detriment of relationships, I know it's time to step forward.

The writing journey traces a similar path. For a good while we move through an interior realm of memories and reflection; we withdraw from our busy lives to enhance our insights and craft stories. Then, at some point, the fruits of the process are too ripe to remain private. These fruits are two-fold—the completed story and what has become of the self as the result of writing. Both press us to leave our safe confines for the dangerous, connective, and gift-giving realm of community.

THE WRITER'S JOURNEY

Before we embark on the obvious journey of making a manuscript public, we will find ourselves on a subtler and more elemental journey—the experience of walking around in the world having written a memoir. During the writing process, the power memories hold over us (defining identity and secretly influencing our emotional responses to present-day events) is released into the manuscript. Eventually we are no longer controlled by the past. Instead, the power of our memories is integrated into our identities. You know who you are. You know where you came from. You know, as best as you are able, what gives your life meaning and continuity. You now own your story in a thorough and dynamic way, and this manifests itself in a personal power that affects your every interaction. This is the inward journey.

The primary outward journey after writing a memoir has to do with your relationship to holiness and to the wider community—your loved ones, neighborhood, co-workers, country, and society. When you know your story, you are less likely to accept the falsehoods others (such as politicians and the advertising industry) tell about you. Knowing your story helps shift the axis of your values away from external systems, such as religious codes of behavior, to the center of your being. The practice of using your voice on the page strengthens the connection between the inner life and language; you grow accustomed to listening to private stirrings and encouraging them to emerge in a more public realm. Lots of traffic between inner and outer worlds widens the road. If we allow it, this road can remain open in other daily dealings—in our spoken voice, in our intimate relationships, in a willingness to take strong moral stands. Having worked extensively with your personal truth, you are better prepared to participate in broader social, political, and spiritual dialogues. If the primary transformation that occurs when writing memoir is the self, then your primary gift to society is that self transformed. The manuscript that makes this possible is just a bonus.

For this reason, the real celebration of our writing should not occur when it is published but when it is complete. Finishing a large writing project can be a letdown if it is a silent, private ending. Mark the completion in some way—a ritual, a party, a quiet moment. I went out and bought myself a Celtic knot ring I'd been eyeing for years. Now, whenever I notice its glint of silver, I do a secret internal victory dance. It reminds me that I know who I am. I know my story.

The power of the past is incorporated into the self as we write and it also becomes embodied in language, where others can access it. It is entirely up to you whether or how much you share your manuscript. Going public is a challenging affair. The question, What will others think? is no longer hypothetical; your intimate story will interact with others' stories in ways beyond your control, leaving you exposed and vulnerable. If you self-publish you face the nit-picking fact finders among your relations, hurt feelings, and sometimes even anger at your story's content. If you send the manuscript to potential agents or publishers, their rejections, although an inevitable part of the publishing process, can feel like a personal affront. If your memoir is published, the publicist's lack of attention, the small sales numbers, bad reviews, or any number of (sadly common) responses can seem devastating. It's a brutal world. One Jewish memoirist in town unlisted his phone number after he received anti-Semitic calls. I don't list my phone number for fear of heterosexist, hyperChristian harassment. Taking a place in the larger public dialogue can be frightening.

As the years have passed since the publication of my first book, however, I've learned an important fact: My memoir is not my self. At first, it is hard to separate the two. (People who hate my book must surely hate me.) But I've changed tremendously since I wrote *Swinging on the Garden Gate*. I no longer agree with everything I claimed then, my writing has smoothed out, and my theology has grown more complex. My memoir is a story exerting its own distinct and separate presence on the world, quite different from my bodily presence. Others' responses to my memoir are caused only in part by my art. Beyond relaying my memories to the best of my abilities, I have no control over—and I am certainly not responsible for—readers' reactions.

There's a school of literary criticism that says the writer is dead, meaning that the real creation happens between text and reader. While this philosophy is extreme (without the writer, the text cannot come into being), there is some truth to it. The reader lays his or her story down in the margins of your story and compares notes, responds with emotions and thoughts, and engages with you to varying degrees. Creative expression continues beyond the completion of a manuscript, but it happens between the manuscript and the reader, leaving the writer entirely out of the loop.

This isn't to say authors can't learn from their mistakes. If you've been careless, cruel, or false in your portrayal of a loved one and lose that person's love as a result, you need to take responsibility for the loss. In a sense one of the gifts of sharing your work is that you learn to be accountable to your community. However, there's a difference between work that misrepresents the truth, thereby generating negative reactions, and work that accurately represents the truth and generates negative reactions. Putting our story into the world requires that we live openly with our truth. This is a profound challenge—one that shifts relationships and allows us to come forward with more integrity than we could have imagined. In *Let Your Life Speak*, Parker Palmer frames this challenge as both spiritual and political: "The punishment imposed on us for claiming true self can never be worse than the punishment we impose on ourselves by failing to make that claim. And the converse is true as well: no reward anyone might give us could possibly be greater than the reward that comes from living by our own best lights." The memoir's journey outward invites us to live "divided no more," which Palmer defines as deciding "no longer to act on the outside in a way that contradicts some truth [that you] hold deeply on the inside." Sharing our writing invites continuity between our internal realm and our external presence. Bold actions like these form the basis of liberation movements; they are the instigators of social change.

Sharing your writing may be difficult, but it is also a great delight. When the words you've labored over so long appear in print or between covers, they seem dressed to the nines. It is grand to feel proud. What was private for so long is now separate, and amazingly competent. Sometimes my book feels like a coveted junior-high hall pass; it gives me permission to step outside the bounds of my private life and meander down public hallways. I interact with people I'd never otherwise have the opportunity to meet. I allow my voice to be heard.

Readers (be they family, friends, or strangers) recognize vulnerability in writing; they gravitate toward genuine quests and are most often extremely grateful. This is particularly true for readers of spiritual memoir. People are so hungry for real accounts of doubt, enlightenment, prayer, and the daily struggle for meaning that they're quite generous in lavishing praise and overlooking a book's faults. I've made marvelous connections with readers and writers from having a published book; my community has widened and strengthened. Openly sharing my spiritual journey has inspired others to share as well—in conversation and in writing. While fame and fortune rarely come to spiritual memoirists, these other, humbler rewards are deeply gratifying.

In the end, though, authors tend to feel a strange remove from the praise others heap on their writing. When I look at my books, I'm astounded that their pages emerged from me. I sweated for years at the computer; I wept and wrote in my journal and scuffled with memories and took determined walks; my fingers typed, revised, and edited each word. And yet I sense that some generative force beyond me is really responsible for the final result. I take in others' compliments, allowing the warmth of their responses to nourish my creative spirit, but then I do my best to let them go—to pass their praise along to the source, where true praise is due.

Writing Practice, Spiritual Practice

WHEN I WAS in my mid-twenties working toward a master of fine arts degree, a fellow student in my memoir class asked an audacious question of the instructor: Did she or did she not believe in God? Without hesitation—and with end-of-discussion curtness—the teacher responded, "Writing is my religion." Enough said. The class went about its business of learning to write well.

But the comment stopped me in my tracks. Writing as religion? At the time, I was heavily enough invested in my local United Methodist church and concrete enough in my theology to take offense. How dare she equate the grueling (albeit glorious) process of working with language to my (obviously more sanctified) belief in God? For months afterward, I composed pages of arguments in my journal defending real faith against the onslaught of secularized concepts of religion. Where's the worship in writing? The moral framework? Doctrine? Image of the divine? Where's the tradition and fellowship that lend identity to religion? It seemed presumptuous for this author to allow writing to usurp the holy place of religion in her life. I was sure Jesus, Mohammed, and the Lord Krishna himself were all turning in their graves, so to speak.

Since that moment my own concept of faith has undergone serious revision; I've come to agree with my graduate teacher, although not without qualifications. *Religion* is too organized a word to describe the lonely grappling of the writing process. As the importance of adhering to a particular belief system has receded in my life, I've come to use the term spiritual practice as a more viable, inclusive, and not-quite-so-uptight way to describe my deliberate attention to sacred presence. I'm convinced that the great mystery fueling the universe is less concerned with moral doctrine and dogma than it is with relationship, and that any means for enriching sacred relationship is welcome. A spiritual practice is any discipline that calls us to attention, brings our truest self into being, and deepens our engagement with the numinous. If showing up for meditation at the zendo does this, great. If writing spiritual memoir does this, why not honor it?

    Write a metaphor that describes your spiritual journey. Perhaps it is like peeling the layers of an onion, walking a labyrinth, or wearing out a pair of shoes. Linger with your metaphor, allowing it to teach you about your spiritual journey.

During my silent, intimate, early hours at the computer—even during small temper tantrums at whole paragraphs gone awry—I know, more clearly than at other moments, a divine presence at work. I recognize it when my hunches for syllables and sounds lead me to words I'm surprised are in my vocabulary. I recognize it at the end of a torturous draft when, after letting it sit for a week, I read through and am shocked by its vitality. I recognize mystery at work when the broken fragments of images and ideas are suddenly smoothed over by transitions, and a piece becomes healthy and plump. When I follow my literary hunches through a written story, I add another chapter to my own lived story. New age writers might say that I'm channeling divine energy on to the page, but in my experience the opposite happens: The writing channels energy into my life so that, at the end of a piece, I'm more awake to the world and more responsive to myself than ever before. It's an awful lot like getting pregnant. On one level we know how a child is conceived, but on another, that spark of life baffles and humbles us. Bringing something from ourselves into being changes us. This new life gives us new life.

When I set out to write my first memoir, I was under the grand illusion that I was writing a book. At least that's what I told myself in order to haul my body out of bed at five-thirty every morning to write before going to teach seventh grade. At the end of six years of work, I had two hundred polished pages to show for it. Halfway through, however, I realized that the book itself was really writing me—that the careful telling of my past, my reflections on sexual identity, and my search for God had softened, shifted, and honed who I was. I wrote about discovering the spirit in my sexuality but found the discovery incomplete until it had been articulated. Every revision brought fresh insight into how holiness inhabits my bodily experiences. By becoming a creator, I found myself being created. We pour energy into our writing, but then there's a feedback loop where we least expect it, and so creative energy flows from our stories back into our personhood. Call it what you will—mystery, God, the muse. It's this stunning dynamic that draws me again and again to the page.

The best evidence I can offer that writing is a spiritual practice is, perversely, what happens when I don't write. Beware! I become a terror. I snap at my friends, refuse to scratch the cat's tummy, and feel bitter toward every book that lines my shelves. I feel trapped inside my skin, as though writing opens pores and releases pent-up waste. The longer I don't write, the less I know what I think or how I feel or what I believe. My breathing turns shallow. My shoulders hunch.

I avoid this horrible state at all costs.

Any spiritual practice that holds potential for an individual has a certain tug. On the surface sitting in silence seems pointless, boring, even insane, but meditators nonetheless feel yanked by silence or tantalized by its elusive, secret treat. I recognize this tug in every student who wants to write. Despite all the nay-saying voices, we must yield to this tug. It is wiser than we are.

Peel the veneer from the craft of writing and you find underneath a structure for spiritual growth. It's all there: The learned habit of openness. The discipline of listening deeply. Letting go of ego in deference to some larger, barely discernible intent. Honoring details as an access to the universal. Facing weakness and brokenness so healing can happen. Shedding illusions and naming what is. Unitive, peak moments; lost-in-the-wilderness moments. Millions of moments lived in ordinary time. Call and response, the quality of prayer. The faith required to begin, to continue, to finish, to share.

    ꙳ Return to your spiritual journey metaphor from the preceding exercise. Apply this same metaphor to your experience of writing. What does the metaphor have to teach you about the writing journey?

When we write spiritual memoir, the content of our writing is our very soul; what strengthens the content also strengthens our being. The ultimate testimony of spiritual memoir is that we each contain, within our life stories, all the material necessary to reveal the source and inspiration of our being. Healing happens at the intersection of event and emotion. With reflection, images disclose their layers of significance. The story itself becomes a container able to hold all the horror and glory of a life. This is the closest I can come to describing my own experience of God—as a container, a story, holding breath and death in unfathomable unity. If Meister Eckhart was right when he said, "Every creature is a word of God and is a book about God," then the best window onto the sacred story is our own. Beneath all spiritual memoir is this common principle: Our stories reveal holiness.

Writing may not be a religion, but it is clearly another means to a similar end. In Sanskrit, the word *shrada* connotes both *imagination* and *faith*. When we leap into the writing process, conjuring and arranging words until they achieve consonance, and imagine our life story on to the printed page, we participate in an act of faith. The exertion of creative energy is, in itself, a witness to holiness. During those rare moments when you connect the creativity within you to the creative energy beyond you—the energy spinning out the universe's story—you know writing as an act of reverence. The temple is the page; the prophet is the pen. The words whispered and echoing in those hallowed halls are only partly of your own making.

For Further Reading

MEMOIRS

Andrew, Elizabeth. *Swinging on the Garden Gate: A Spiritual Memoir.* Boston: Skinner House Books, 2000.

Augustine. *The Confessions of St. Augustine.* New York: Doubleday, 1960.

Black Elk. *Black Elk Speaks.* As told to John Neihardt. Lincoln: University of Nebraska Press, 1932.

Bondi, Roberta. *Memories of God: Theological Reflections on a Life.* Nashville: Abingdon, 1995.

Bozarth, Alla Renee. *Womanpriest: A Personal Odyssey.* San Diego: LuraMedia, 1978.

Breyer, Chloe. *The Close: A Young Woman's First Year at Seminary.* New York: Basic Books, 2000.

Chernin, Kim. *In My Father's Garden: A Daughter's Search for a Spiritual Life.* Chapel Hill, NC: Algonquin Books, 1996.

Covington, Dennis. *Salvation on Sand Mountain*. New York: Penguin, 1995.

Crane, George. *Bones of the Master: A Buddhist Monk's Search for the Lost Heart of China*. New York: Bantam, 2000.

David-Neel, Alexandra. *My Journey to Lhasa*. Boston: Beacon Press, 1927.

Doty, Mark. *Heaven's Coast*. New York: Harper Perennial, 1996.

Doyle, Brian. "Eating Dirt," in *The Best Spiritual Writing 1999*, ed. Philip Zaleski. New York: HarperSanFrancisco, 1999.

Dubus, Andre. "Love in the Morning," in *The Best Spiritual Writing 1998*, ed. Philip Zaleski. New York: HarperSanFrancisco, 1998.

Duncan, David James. *My Story as Told by Water: Confessions, Druidic Rants, Reflections, Bird-Watchings, Fish-Stalkings, Visions, Songs and Prayers Refracting Light, from Living Rivers, in the Age of the Industrial Dark*. San Francisco: Sierra Club Books, 2002.

Ehrlich, Gretel. *A Match to the Heart: One Woman's Story of Being Struck by Lightning*. New York: Penguin Books, 1994.

Foster, Patricia. *Minding the Body: Women Writers on Body and Soul*. New York: Doubleday, 1994.

Frank, Anne. *The Diary of Anne Frank*. New York: Doubleday, 1989.

Gallagher, Winifred. *Working on God*. New York: Random House, 1999.

Gaustad, Edwin S., ed. *Memoirs of the Spirit*. Grand Rapids, MI: Eerdmans, 1999.

Goldberg, Natalie. *Long Quiet Highway*. New York: Bantam Books, 1993.

Halpern, Sue. *Migrations to Solitude: The Quest for Privacy in a Crowded World*. New York: Vintage Books, 1992.

Hampl, Patricia. *Virgin Time*. New York: Ballantine Books, 1992.

Harvey, Andrew. *A Journey in Ladakh*. Boston: Houghton Mifflin, 1983.

Hathaway, Katharine Butler. *The Little Locksmith*. New York: The Feminist Press, 1942.

Hendra, Tony. *Father Joe: The Man Who Saved My Soul*. New York: Random House, 2004.

Hillesum, Etty. *An Interrupted Life*. New York: Pocket Books, 1981.

Johnson, Robert A. *Balancing Heaven and Earth: A Memoir of Visions, Dreams, and Realizations*. San Francisco: HarperSanFrancisco, 1998.

Jung, Carl. *Memories, Dreams, Reflections*. New York: Vintage Books, 1961.

Junod, Tom. "Can You Say Hero?" in *The Best Spiritual Writing 1999*, ed. Philip Zaleski. New York: HarperSanFrancisco, 1999.

Kamenetz, Rodger. *The Jew in the Lotus: A Poet's Rediscovery of Jewish Identity in Buddhist India*. New York: HarperSanFrancisco, 1994.

Kempe, Margery. *The Book of Margery Kempe*. New York: Penguin, 1985.

Kingston, Maxine Hong. *The Woman Warrior: Memoirs of a Girlhood Among Ghosts*. New York: Vintage Books, 1975.

Kurs, Katherine, ed. *Searching for Your Soul: Writers of Many Faiths Share Their Personal Stories of Spiritual Discovery*. New York: Shocken Books, 1999.

Lamott, Anne. *Traveling Mercies: Some Thoughts on Faith*. New York: Anchor Books, 2000.

Lee, Li-Young. *The Winged Seed: A Remembrance*. St. Paul, MN: Hungry Mind Find, 1995.

Levine, Stephen. *Turning Toward the Mystery: A Seeker's Journey*. New York: HarperSanFrancisco, 2002.

Macy, Joanna. *Widening Circles*. Gabriola Island, BC: New Society Publishers, 2000.

Mairs, Nancy. *Ordinary Time: Cycles in Marriage, Faith, and Renewal*. Boston: Beacon Press, 1993.

Manning, Martha. *Chasing Grace: Reflections of a Catholic Girl, Grown Up*. San Francisco: HarperCollins, 1996.

Matthiessen, Peter. *The Snow Leopard*. New York: Penguin, 1978.

Mernissi, Fatima. *Dreams of Trespass: Tales of a Harem Girlhood*. Boulder, CO: Perseus Books, 1994.

Merton, Thomas. *Seven Storey Mountain*. New York: Harcourt Brace and Co., 1948.

Momaday, N. Scott. *The Names*. Tucson: The University of Arizona Press, 1976.

———. *The Way to Rainy Mountain*. Albuquerque: University of New Mexico Press, 1969.

Morrison, Melanie. *The Grace of Coming Home*. Cleveland: Pilgrim Press, 1995.

Norris, Kathleen. *Dakota: A Spiritual Geography*. Boston: Houghton Mifflin, 1993.

Nouwen, Henri. *The Genesee Diary: Report from a Trappist Monastery*. New York: Doubleday & Co., Inc., 1976.

O'Reilly, Mary Rose. *Barn at the End of the World: The Apprenticeship of a Quaker, Buddhist Shepherd*. Minneapolis: Milkweed, 2001.

Rosen, Jonathan. *The Talmud and the Internet: A Journey Between Worlds*. New York: Farrar, Straus, and Giroux, 2000.

Rothluebber, Francis. *Nobody Owns Me: A Celibate Woman Discovers Her Sexual Power*. San Diego: LuraMedia, 1994.

Sandor, Marjorie. "Waiting for a Miracle: A Jew Goes Fishing," in *The Best Spiritual Writing 2000*, ed. Philip Zaleski. New York: Harper-SanFrancisco, 2000.

Sarton, May. *Journal of a Solitude*. New York: W.W. Norton, 1973.

Teresa of Avila. *The Life of Saint Teresa of Avila by Herself*. London: Penguin Books, 1957.

Tweedie, Irina. *Chasm of Fire*. Dorset, England: Element Books, 1979.

Wiesel, Elie. *Night*. New York: Avon, 1969.

Williams, Terry Tempest. *Refuge*. New York: Vintage Books, 1991.

Willis, Jan. *Dreaming Me: An African American Woman's Spiritual Journey*. New York: Riverhead Books, 2001.

Winner, Lauren. *Girl Meets God: On the Path to a Spiritual Life*. Chapel Hill, NC: Algonquin Books, 2002.

Wurtele, Margaret. *Touching the Edge: A Mother's Spiritual Path from Loss to Life*. Hoboken, NJ: John Wiley, 2003.

Zaleski, Philip, ed. *The Best Spiritual Writing*, annual series. New York: HarperSanFrancisco.

RESOURCES FOR WRITING

Ackerman, Diane. *Natural History of the Senses*. New York: Vintage Books, 1990.

Baines, Barry K. *The Ethical Will Resource Kit: Preserving Your Legacy of Values for Your Family*. Minneapolis: Josaba Ltd., 1998.

Bayles, David and Ted Orland. *Art and Fear*. Consortium Books, 2001.

Bly, Carol. *Beyond the Writer's Workshop: New Ways to Write Creative Nonfiction*. New York: Anchor Books, 2001.

Cameron, Julia. *The Artist's Way: A Spiritual Path to Higher Creativity*. New York: G. P. Putnam's Sons, 1992.

DeSalvo, Louise. *Writing as a Way of Healing*. Boston: Beacon, 1999.

Dillard, Annie. *The Writing Life*. New York: HarperCollins, 1989.

Hampl, Patricia. "Memory and Imagination" in *I Could Tell You Stories: Sojourns in the Land of Memory*. New York: Norton, 1999.

Lerner, Betsy. *The Forest for the Trees: An Editor's Advice to Writers*. New York: Riverhead Books, 2001.

Norris, Kathleen. "Words and the Word." *Christian Century*, April 16, 1997.

Riemer, Jack. *Ethical Wills: Putting Your Values on Paper*. Boulder, CO: Perseus Publishing, 2001.

Rosen, Jonathan. "A Retreat from the World Can Be a Perilous Journey," *The New York Times*, May 7, 2001.

Shulevit, Judith. "In God They Trust, Sort Of," *The New York Times Book Review*, August 25, 2002.

Skinner, Jeffery. "Push Hands: Balancing Resistance and Revision," *Poets and Writers*, May-June, 2002.

Ueland, Brenda. *If You Want to Write: A Book about Art, Independence, and Spirit*. St. Paul, MN: Graywolf, 1987.

Zaleski, Philip. "God Help the Spiritual Writer," *The New York Times Book Review*, January 10, 1999.

Zinsser, William. *Inventing the Truth: The Art and Craft of Memoir*. Boston: Houghton Mifflin Company, 1998.

———. *Spiritual Quests: The Art and Craft of Religious Writing*. Boston: Houghton Mifflin Company, 1988.

WORKS QUOTED

Cooper, Bernard. *Truth Serum*. Boston: Houghton Mifflin, 1996.

Dillard, Annie. *An American Childhood*. New York: HarperPerennial, 1987.

———. *Holy the Firm*. New York: Harper and Row, 1977.

———. *Pilgrim at Tinker Creek*. New York: Harper's Magazine Press, 1974.

Earley, Tony. *Somehow Form a Family*. Chapel Hill, NC: Algonquin Books, 2001.

Fowler, James. *Stages of Faith: The Psychology of Human Development and the Quest for Meaning*. New York: HarperSanFrancisco, 1995.

Fox, Matthew. *Original Blessing*. Santa Fe, NM: Bear & Co., 1983.

Hurston, Zora Neale. *Their Eyes Were Watching God*. New York: Perennial Classics, 1937.

———. "How It Feels to Be Colored Me," *World Tomorrow*, Vol. 11 (May 1928).

Moore, Thomas. *Care of the Soul: A Guide for Cultivating Depth and Sacredness in Everyday Life*. New York: HarperPerennial, 1992.

Palmer, Parker. *Let Your Life Speak: Listening for the Voice of Vocation*. San Francisco: Jossey Bass, 2000.

Sanders, Scott Russell. "Amos and James" in *The Force of Spirit*. Boston: Beacon Press, 2000.

———. "Under the Influence," in *The Art of the Personal Essay*, ed. Phillip Lopate. New York: Anchor Books, 1995.

Simpkinson, Charles and Anne Simpkinson. *Sacred Stories: A Celebration of the Power of Stories to Transform and Heal*. New York: HarperSanFrancisco, 1993.

Touré. "What's Inside You, Brother?" in *The Best American Essays 1999*, ed. Edward Hoagland. Boston: Houghton Mifflin, 1999.

Acknowledgments

OVER THE PAST TEN YEARS, I have had the honor of working with hundreds of beginning writers—on retreats, in churches, at The Loft Literary Center in Minneapolis, Minnesota, and in my home. These courageous and earnest people have taught me far more than I ever taught them. I have read their most intimate stories, from which I have discovered much about patterns in the spirit's life and in learning to write well. *Writing the Sacred Journey* has its origin in these students' efforts to grow as human beings and writers. I thank them all.

I would like to acknowledge a few individuals who contributed ideas and insights directly to this book. I appreciate Lisa Dietz for her wisdom regarding writing about trauma, especially "writing in the negative space." Thanks to Wally Conhaim for sending me information on ethical wills, and to Dosho Port, Julie Neraas, and Mary Bednarowski for their book recommendations. I am grateful to Lauri Wollner, Dale Korogi, and Rachel Gaffron for permission to use examples from their writing, and to many others whose process inspired the examples I created. Gratitude of an increasing longevity goes to my mentors at Hamline University, whose instruction continues to prove solid, and to Patricia Hampl, whose work with memoir has influenced me greatly.

As always, I am indebted to my writing group—Marcia Peck, Carolyn Crooke, and Terri Whitman—for the numerous hours they have invested in my work. I am also grateful to Christine Sikorski, poet and neighbor, whose careful reading tightened my prose. What would I do without you friends?

Gratitude also goes to The Loft for promoting and hosting my spiritual memoir classes. *The View From the Loft* published an early article of mine ("Faith in Writing," October 2000) that served as a springboard for this book.

Thanks to Kristen Blue for feeding me popcorn on retreat while I pushed through my initial draft, and to Emily Hughes for cheerleading my "miritual spemoir" in many a midmorning e-mail. As always, I appreciate my sister's willingness to be written about and my family's enduring support.

Finally, my sincere thanks to Mary Benard for suggesting I write this book and for providing a venue through Skinner House. It wouldn't have happened without your encouragement.